MAD DOGS & ME

A COMEDY DIARY

SAZ WILSON

Gentle Giant Press

First published in 2024 by Gentle Giant Press

ISBN 978-1-7384647-0-8

Dedicated to:

All the unloved animals out there.

And all of you readers who are helping me save them.

A NOTE FROM SAZ

Firstly, a HUGE thank you for buying Mad Dogs & Me. The reason I wrote this book was to make people laugh and to raise money to open an animal sanctuary. I hope to achieve both these goals, or if not, at least one!

Everything in this book happened, but some people's names and identifying features, and certain locations have been changed to protect their privacy.

Nothing in this book is meant to offend anyone but it's inevitable in comedic writing that someone gets offended. I'm sorry if that's you – please don't cancel me.

No animals were harmed in the writing of this book (a few might have been traumatised but I think they're okay now).

Happy reading!

Love

Saz x

CONTENTS

CHAPTER 1 – AUGUST

THE CALM BEFORE THE STORM

Saturday 4 August

We're getting a dog! When I say we, I mean me, as I haven't actually relayed this information to the family yet. I realise this might be an adjustment given that we've had cats for the past twenty years but now that our "quiet residential street" has become a rat run and we've lost all three of our beloved cats to hit-and-run drivers, I can't take another loss.

I'm currently Googling, "dogs that don't kill cats" as the plan is to rescue more cats when we eventually move. I'm surprised at how many dogs would like a cat for breakfast so will continue the search until I find a breed with a compatible, gentle nature.

Important characteristics for our new family member must include:

1. Good with kids (would like children to keep all limbs)
2. Doesn't eat cats (obviously)
3. Intelligent (easy to train)
4. Doesn't moult (hate housework)
5. Good looking (I mean, who wants an ugly dog)
6. Size of dog – medium to large (to be discussed with husband)

Sunday 5 August

Announced the news to Ella who, like any eight-year-old child, is yelping with excitement. The husband not so much. He assumed when I said we need a pet we can contain, I meant a hamster or a guinea pig. However, after much persuasion, he has given in and said he will consider getting a small lap dog.

Have decided not to mention I'm not a small dog person until he is fully on board with the whole getting-a-dog idea.

Monday 6 August

It's too noisy to get any work done with the constant banging and crashing of building work going on. Who knew a simple extension could take so long! But with Ella at theatre club, it gives me a free day to browse suitable dog breeds instead.

Five hours later and I've found exactly what we're looking for. A Rhodesian Ridgeback, AKA an African Lion Dog! Although it's not exactly a small dog, weighing in at a possible 50 kilos when fully grown, it does like cats so that's a bonus! Other plus points include: highly intelligent, loyal and protective, and loves exercise. The downside is they can be stubborn, difficult to train, don't really like other dogs and are the size of a human. Might not mention those to Ivan just yet.

Although I've not had extensive dog experience in recent years, we did have a Dulux dog when I was a kid so I do have some knowledge of large breeds. I absolutely loved our dog, Ben. He would sit next to me on the sofa and rest his head on my shoulder like a friend. Although he was bigger than me, he was such a gentle giant. Not the brightest spark, but what he lacked in brains, he made up for with love. I recognise that getting a large dog might take some convincing, but I'm sure Ivan will understand.

Tuesday 7 August

'You know absolutely NOTHING about large dogs!'

This wasn't entirely true. I explained my backstory, emphasising that I was the one who took Ben for walks before school and at weekends, and that he slept with me on my bed and was no trouble at all. Admittedly, I didn't mention that Ben used to pull me flat on my face and knock me flying whenever he jumped up. Then I played my trump card and told him it would be such a lovely companion for Ella, especially as she's an only child. I could see the cogs turning and assured Ivan that big dogs don't yap and are a good deterrent for burglars.

'I will train him and be really strict with him,' I said. 'Besides, it's no more work than getting a small dog,' although I had no idea if this was actually true.

I don't remember Ben being particularly hard work but I was only nine at the time so my memory might be a bit foggy.

Wednesday 8 August

Unbelievably, just five miles away was a family whose dog had just given birth to a litter of Ridgeback puppies. What were the odds? They were a young couple who'd allowed their family dog to mate with a friend's dog. They weren't experienced breeders and just wanted their puppies to go to responsible families where one person worked from home and had a garden big enough for them to run around in. It was fate. We had a huge garden and we *both* worked from home! I called immediately and arranged to see the puppies first thing Friday. Ella and I could barely contain our excitement. Strangely, Ivan could.

Friday 10 August

Since Ivan was not impressed at the thought of living with a dog who would be bigger than our daughter and stronger than him, I thought the best plan of action would be to take him to see the puppies to win him over.

We rang the doorbell and were greeted by the deep bark of an obviously very large dog. Trying not to look alarmed, we entered the kitchen where a huge playpen, taking up most of the floor, was filled with tiny sleepy puppies piled on top of one another – all thirteen of them! Their mother was shut in the room next door, presumably not to scare the living daylights out of potential adopters.

It was hard to grasp that these chubby, comatose puppies would grow into large athletic dogs. They were only two weeks old but were already absolutely beautiful. Their coats were a shiny chestnut auburn with a clear ridge running all the way down their backs. I didn't realise the ridge was just their hair growing in the opposite direction. Their plump pink tummies, huge paws and tiny floppy ears made them even more adorable than I was expecting. And I could see Ivan melting right before my eyes. The plan was working.

'You need to choose who you want today,' E said. I was slightly taken aback given that they were so young and looked identical, except for their different coloured collars.

'Don't I need to get to know them first to see if we're compatible?' I asked. Ivan raised an eyebrow and I realised this sounded more like I was enquiring at a dating agency, but I'd heard this was true.

'I've got three families coming later today and five more tomorrow,' she said. 'Four puppies have already gone.' I was about to add that I thought dogs were meant to choose *us* but realised that as most of them hadn't opened their eyes yet, this was a moot point given that they couldn't actually see us. But inexperienced breeder or not, there was no better sales tactic than thinking you were going to end up with the runt of the litter.

'I definitely want a boy,' I blurted out.

'Most people want boys as they're bigger,' said E, and she handed me a tiny, bleary-eyed pup with a white collar. I held him close, he nuzzled into me and I fell instantly in love.

Across the room, Ella had also fallen in love, but with a different puppy – a pretty little girl in an orange collar. This puppy was bright and alert, wriggling away and very vocal. Ivan had also fallen for her.

'Your one is dopey and will be impossible to train. We should get this one,' Ivan said.

'He's only two weeks old!' I snapped but worried that if this was true, would I be able to handle a lifetime of Ivan's "I told you so" quips. I didn't want to make the wrong decision and so we agreed that I could come back tomorrow by myself to make my final decision. Ivan looked relieved as he secretly hoped I wouldn't pick any of them.

Later that night I sent a text to E in a panic. 'If someone chooses Otis, can you call me right away.' And that was it. Like a farmer naming one of his flock, the puppy's fate was sealed. He was coming home with me.

Saturday 11 August

Ella woke up overjoyed about the prospect of getting a puppy and followed up with a barrage of questions. 'Are you going to see the puppies today? Can I come? Are you getting the little girl?' I explained that I needed to make a clear-headed decision as I was the one responsible for the puppy when he or she came home, and so today, I was going alone. I didn't mention the message I'd sent last night. As I left, Ivan couldn't resist reminding me that the girl was clever and the boy was a dope.

As soon as I walked in, Otis came waddling up to me and I almost burst into tears. He chose me! It was such a relief knowing I'd made the right decision, but then little orange collar trotted over to me, flopped onto my lap and went to sleep. She was ridiculously beautiful. I looked at E, helpless.

'You could take them both,' she said. 'I'll give you a discount.'

She gushed about how happy they would be if they went together and how quickly they would settle in, how they'd never be lonely and wouldn't miss their mother. I was tempted, but I wasn't insane. She told me she was keeping one of the puppies to be company for Jasmine, their mother, and I asked if I could meet Jasmine. She was bloody massive! She wasn't a dog; she was a pony! Perhaps getting a boy who would be even bigger might not be such a great idea after all.

'You really need to decide today who you want as they'll both be gone this week.'

The pressure! Do I get the boy and risk him being a bit slow? Do I get the girl and regret not getting him? Should I just get them both? I was all over the place. So much for being clear headed.

E suggested I call Ivan to see what he thought about getting both of them. It didn't take a rocket scientist to figure out what Ivan would think, but I snuck into the garden to make the call and work my magic charm.

'ABSOLUTELY NO FUCKING WAY!'

'But I can't decide,' I pleaded.

'Then don't get either!' he unhelpfully added.

'But they'll keep each other company when we go out,' I whined.

'NO!'

I paid the deposit for both and drove home feeling sick.

Sunday 12 August

Thinking I'd better get fully prepared before bringing two large puppies home next month and avoiding a divorce, I did some research regarding training sibling puppies, otherwise known as litter mates.

The first headline read: *Two puppies from the same litter – the worst of both worlds!*

The second: *Never get two puppies from the same litter as they will be impossible to train. They will bond together and turn on you.*

And the third: *Always get the second puppy a year after training the first so it can learn the good behaviour from them. NEVER get litter mates as they will copy each other's bad behaviour and you will never know who is responsible for the destruction.*

Search after search revealed problem after problem, issue after issue, including pack mentality, disrespect for humans and aggression towards other dogs. The list was startling.

As mild panic set in, I called a top dog trainer for advice, hoping for the voice of reason.

'Give one back now before it's too late,' he said without

hesitation. 'You will never be able to cope with two high-energy puppies. It will be impossible to manage them and you will end up rehoming one. Life will be unbearable.'

With the level of panic now rising, I made a mental note not to pass any of this information on to Ivan whilst pouring myself a very large glass of wine.

I logged onto Amazon and bought every puppy-training manual available.

I poured a second glass of wine and booked puppy-training sessions for the week they arrive.

I poured a third glass of wine and ordered a stack of dog-psychology books.

As the wine flooded my system and my panic subsided, I repeated the mantra, *everything is going to be fine.* They're just dogs, for goodness' sake. I mean, how hard can it be?

Monday 13 August

I woke at 5 a.m. with a hangover, mild anxiety and no time to waste. I went straight onto YouTube and watched back-to-back training videos by a renowned American dog expert. I made studious notes on recall, lead training, toilet training and crate training. Extremely pleased with my colour-coded notetaking, I'd almost filled an entire notepad before breakfast.

The heavy thud of dog-training books arrived and the entire week is pencilled in for reading and studying all aspects of puppy training. Work will have to wait. This could be tricky as I work for Ivan but I think he'll understand that puppy knowledge is more important than architecture right now. Clients will have to wait a week for their invoices. I don't think they'll complain. I continue watching training videos by the dog expert well into the night and complete my notebook with all his golden nuggets of advice before starting on my pile of puppy-training books.

The first book says not to do anything this dog expert says as his methods are cruel and outdated. Training must be reward-based and not punitive. I watch back some of the videos and realise that they are probably cruel as I've now learnt that frantic tail wagging is not excitement but massive stress. I chuck my colour-coded notebook in the bin, order a book on dog body language and switch to the Essential Puppy Book instead, for a softer approach.

Saturday 18 August

We are off to see the pups now they are four weeks old. Ella has named the little girl Kiara, after Simba and Nala's cub in the Lion King, which is kind of apt considering they are lion dogs. Ella is coming with me but Ivan is still sulking. He almost admitted to liking the name Otis as we both love Otis Redding (and the puppy's coat is red, sort of), but for now he needs to maintain his air of superiority about the fact that I am absolutely doing the wrong thing (which, according to every expert, I am), and is therefore having no part of it.

We're both shocked at how much the pups have grown in just two weeks! Otis is outside the pen and comes tottering over as soon as he sees us. Kiara is in the pen and is borderline manic. Jasmine is free-roaming now that E has our deposit and there's no turning back. When Kiara spots her mum, she tramples over her siblings, clambers out of the pen and drops into a heap on the floor. She charges over to Jasmine and grabs a teat. Jasmine knocks her off with her goliath-sized paw and Ella scoops Kiara up and puts her on her lap. Kiara then proceeds to pull off every pompom on Ella's favourite skirt. This puppy is feral compared to Otis who lies quietly in my arms, gazing up at me. His eyes are fully open now and he is absolutely gorgeous. I don't believe for a second this dog is dopey.

I use this opportunity to drop into conversation about the litter-mates issue, i.e., that my life will shortly be over! E looks genuinely surprised. She says she's never heard this before and tells me not to worry. I perhaps foolishly believe her. Right now, I need to hang on to any shred of hope because they're coming home with us in four weeks, besides, no one in their right mind would recommend taking siblings if it was that bad.

Sunday 19 August

Essential Puppy List:

- Crates (to keep them safe when unsupervised and to be their den for comfort)
- Mattress
- Blankets
- Fleeces to cover crates
- Food bowls
- Water bowl
- Playpen
- Baby gate
- Collars
- ID tags
- Harnesses
- Leads (short, medium and long)
- Brushes
- Shampoo
- Large towels
- Poo bags
- Chew toys

- Play toys – balls, ropes, etc.
- Bones
- Food
- Treats
- Insurance

There are more items on the Essential Puppy List than when I was expecting my first baby! And everything is going to be times two! For the quality items, including their crates, mattresses and bedding, I will go to the top-notch store, and for all the others I will head down to the local superstore so that we're not bankrupt before the pups arrive.

The very helpful shop assistant shows me the crates recommended for large breeds which look enormous.

'What's their weight when fully grown?' she asks.

'They can get up to 50 kilos apparently,' I say, trying to keep the panic out of my voice.

As her eyes widen, she says, 'Wait here,' and disappears out the back.

She returns holding the big guns.

'This is what you need. The extra-large crates.'

As she assembles one, it looks more like a shipping container than a cosy den.

'Are you sure these are the right size? The dogs are really small at the moment.'

'Oh, definitely. Puppies grow really quickly and if you get the smaller one, you'll need to size up in a couple of months.' A COUPLE OF MONTHS?! Christ! I hope they don't fill those crates in a couple of months! However, I err on the side of caution and agree it would be silly to spend this amount of money twice. I can always stuff them with pillows to pad them out in the meantime. As I can only fit one crate into my car – and that's flat packed – I call Ivan to help me out. I hide the bill as I head off with a different credit card to the next store to buy all the other items on the list. I just hope Ella hasn't grown out of her school uniform as we'll only be able to afford new socks at this rate.

Monday 20 August

I've been so busy preparing for the arrival of the pups that I almost forgot we're going on holiday today! Fortunately, I only have to pack for Ella and me as Ivan is staying home to oversee the final leg of the kitchen extension. It's the hottest summer on record so it's probably better weather here than in Los Angeles anyway.

His beloved garden is clearly loving this heatwave. It's lusher than any other time in the five years we've been living here and our tropical plants are the size of triffids. The pups are going to have a ball in this garden. Thank God Ridgebacks aren't diggers or Ivan would be filing for divorce before the dirt had even landed.

I'm praying that the extension, which we were told would be finished in July, is done by the time we get back. A house full of builders and the arrival of two new puppies does not fill me with joy. The taxi arrives just as the deafening crash of a builder's foot appears through the hallway ceiling. There is plaster everywhere. 'Ooooh shiiiit!' he yells. Yes, oh shit indeed.

Tuesday 28 August

We arrive home from holiday in a fog of jet lag. Judging by the state of the house, it looks like the builders also went away as there's still masses to do, including the gaping hole in the ceiling. I dump our cases down and throw a mountain of dirty washing in the laundry room when an ear-piercing sound screeches through the house.

'They're cutting the slate roof tiles today.' Ivan shouts. 'Probably best if you go out for the day.'

'How long 'til this is all finished?' I ask through gritted teeth.

'Probably another two weeks,' he bellows. Which is builder's code for at least another month.

'But the pups arrive on the 9th!' He can't hear me as we're both deafened by the ear-splitting sound of the slate-cutter. 'This means we'll have to turn the living room into the dogs' space until the kitchen is ready,' I shout.

'We'll probably have to put the dogs in the living room until the kitchen is ready,' he shouts back.

God almighty.

Thursday 30 August

The sound of slate tiles being cut is a noise so hideous there is no actual word for it in the English language. It is torturous. With the list of things to do for the pups getting longer the more I seem to do, and the inability to concentrate on anything with this noise, I decide to throw caution to the wind and take Ella out for the day instead. A girlie day in London – shopping, eating and having fun before school starts and I'm housebound with the pups while they settle in – is the perfect tonic.

Ella's excitement for the puppies is contagious as she buys a little squeaky hedgehog toy for Kiara and a little mouse for Otis. They were a bargain at £20 each from Liberty. I hope the dogs appreciate my daughter's expensive taste in knick-knacks.

Friday 31 August

It's the final weekend before the pups arrive, and a builder-free day (no idea where they are) makes it the perfect opportunity to lay our little cat, Nala, to rest. Her ashes have been sitting in the living room for three months.

Ella chose a beautiful mimosa tree and a pink pot to put it in. We scattered Nala's ashes in with the compost and planted the tree. Ella read out a poem written on a picture she'd drawn with all three of our beloved cats wearing halos, now together in heaven. After a lifetime of having cats, it feels like the end of an era.

We laugh at how Nala would have loved to dig in the pot and scratch the branches bare. Ella chose Nala and she was a gorgeous kitten – beautiful and bonkers. She loved our garden with all the trees and would leap between them like a monkey. It is the perfect place to lay her to rest. I feel cheated that she was only with us for two years and am confident that getting dogs is the right thing to do. At least we can keep a dog safe.

We placed the tree on the sunny side of the garden with my roses and I remembered when Ivan had said he didn't want a cat. But then he slept downstairs on the sofa for the first two nights, Nala sleeping on his chest, so that she wasn't lonely in her new home. Although he's not on board yet, I'm sure it won't take long for him to fall in love with the pups either.

As I transfer the balance of money to E, my hand hovers over the send button. My stomach lurches and I feel like I'm sealing my fate. All I can do is hope that what I've read isn't true.

CHAPTER 2 – SEPTEMBER

GREAT EXPECTATIONS

Sunday 9 September – THE PUPS ARRIVE!
(also Dad's birthday, mustn't forget in all the excitement)

I can't believe the pups are coming home today! We're collecting them at 11 a.m., which feels like an eternity given we've been up since 6 a.m. with excitement.

The living room has been temporarily turned into their new den with their shipping containers/beds filling one side of an entire wall. Their plush new bedding is washed and ready in their crates, towels laid down for toilet training and a whole array of puppy toys for chewing, chasing and pulling are scattered around the floor. Their water bowl, so heavy I can barely lift it, is by their beds and most importantly, the baby gate is up so they can't escape.

Ivan thinks I've gone completely overboard, reminding me that "in the wild" these lion dogs would not be chasing a squeaky hedgehog and sleeping on a plush mattress with matching blankets.

Apart from the sofa (which the pups are banned from), and my pink chair, all other furniture has been moved into the kitchen. I didn't want our Balinese dining table, which we bought on our honeymoon, to be mistaken for a giant chew toy.

We arrive early to pick them up and hide around the corner in the car, like some mad family stakeout. As the clock strikes 11 we bolt out of the car, tripping over each other.

We gasp out loud when we see them. They already look the size of a fully-grown dog! Otis is 7.5 kilos and Kiara 6.5 kilos at just eight weeks old. We're the second family to collect our pups and I feel awful taking them away from E and her boyfriend, like I'm some kind of evil dog snatcher. They cuddle them for one last time and I take a photo of them as they hold our new babies and well up with tears. It takes all my effort not to cry with them.

'I'm so glad they're going together,' E says. And I feel exactly the same way.

I ask if Jasmine wants to see them go so she doesn't wonder where they are later, and they say, 'Nah, she's in the other room and can't wait to get rid of them.' Mind you, having thirteen giant puppies chasing your nipples all day, can't say I blame her.

After a failed attempt at getting their new harnesses on, which are already too small for them, we put them in our old cat basket and lugged them to the car. We can't put them down outside until they have their final vaccination so we'd better get used to hauling two big lugs around. I thought the basket handle was going to break off with the weight of them as I'm sure even the most obese cat couldn't weigh anywhere near 14 kilos.

As we drive home, they are squeaking away in the back whilst Ella chats to them.

'Where's Otis's white collar?' Ella asks.

I turn around and see Kiara is still wearing her orange collar, but Otis doesn't have his on.

'It must have come off,' I say.

'It's not in the basket,' she says. It must have come off when she was at E's. God, I hope we've got the right dog.

'Never mind. They're too small for them now anyway. We have two lovely new ones for them when we get home.'

At home…

Having accumulated hundreds of hours in puppy training, I am now a seasoned dog trainer, in theory anyway, and explain crate instructions to the family before we enter the house. The whole point is to get the pups used to the crates in their own time so they love being in them. They should feel safe and cosy, and not scared.

1. Leave the door of the crate open so pups can get used to seeing it
2. Put treats inside to encourage them to enter, followed by massive praise
3. Continue to do this for first day
4. Close door when pups inside, but don't lock it so they can get out by themselves
5. Lock door and give them treats then let them out after one minute
6. Continue doing this for the next five days, gradually increasing the time until they are happy to be in there alone before locking the door

We enter the house and the pups trot straight into their crates, curl up and fall asleep. I ignore the smug look on Ivan's face.

My phone is ringing off the hook. I've not been this popular since giving birth. I allow some friends to come and meet the pups, but unbeknownst to me, Ivan has also done the same thing, and after fourteen sets of visitors, we are all completely shattered, and so are the pups.

After the final visitors leave, Kiara starts throwing up. She won't drink any water and by 9 p.m. I'm worried and call the emergency vets. They think she may have eaten something in the garden and after an anti-nausea shot, fluids and a big hit on my credit card. I take her home. I put both pups into their crates and go to bed, exhausted. It was not the night I'd envisaged with the pups. After fifteen minutes of whimpering, crying and then barking, I grab my duvet and lie down next to them until they settle to sleep.

Every time I creep out, Kiara clocks me and starts crying. In the end, I give in and lie next to them for the night. At least not sleeping made it a lot easier for me to get up at 3 a.m. and let them out for a wee. Oh crap, is it too late to call my dad to wish him a happy birthday?

Monday 10 September

There is more conflicting advice about toilet training puppies than there is for toddlers. If you use puppy pads they'll think it's okay to wee in the house, but if you don't use them your house may be submerged in urine within a matter of hours. I was in the unique position of having two puppies with totally opposite toilet needs. Otis has a bladder the size of a ladybird's and needs to go every three seconds, whereas Kiara is like a camel and can hold it for hours. Therefore, I decided to do *both* methods simultaneously. This meant encouraging both puppies to come outside every hour on the hour and if they did a wee, I would give a fanfare of praise, but if they did it on the pad indoors, I would ignore it.

So far, Otis comes running outside, watches Kiara do a wee and get her treat, then goes trotting indoors and wees on the pad. His constant need to go has created a lagoon-like puddle in the living room and I'm getting through more towels than a hotel spa. Not to mention the fact that I have done absolutely nothing all day other than stand in the garden or mop up wee. Ivan questions whether the current plan is working. I question whether he would like to wear his dinner tonight.

Tuesday 11 September

Ella starts Year 4 today so I get the dogs up early and take them into the garden for a wee. Mornings are not quite the zen-like calm they once were. They exit their crates like two rockets. In the excitement of seeing me, and the fact that I can't get the door open fast enough, they wee all over the floor and my feet. I must remember to open the patio door *before* I let them out of their crates.

Outside, they chase each other around the trees like a couple of lunatics and across the flower beds, de-capitating my begonias as they go. I am impressed at how quickly they have learnt, "ready, steady, GO!" and how they watch me with rapture when I say this, running exactly on the cue "GO" with joyous abandon.

They have absolutely no interest in playing with any of the toys I've drained my savings on and already the expensive Liberty toys are MIA. The tunnel for them to run through has been dragged under one of the pine trees, squashed flat and is covered in mud, and the garish neon rubber balls are all sitting on the lawn like fallen radioactive apples, untouched. The playpen is not fit for purpose as they can jump straight out of it and use it instead to hide behind and pounce on each other as they tear around it in circles. They do love my flowerpots and gardening gloves, though, and fight over these. I've realised there's no point in getting doubles of anything as they only want what the other one has. The second Otis runs off with something in his mouth, Kiara is determined to snatch it off him. She wrestles Otis to the ground, grabs him by the ear and drags him along the lawn yelping until he can't take it anymore, just to show him who's boss. Although he's bigger and stronger than her, she wears the trousers and at times he looks shit-scared of her. I've checked his ears for puncture wounds and so far, so good. At least I've bought top pet insurance should his ears need to be sewn back on.

Ella is so excited to wake up to two puppies which is great news as it usually takes a foghorn to wake her up in the mornings. Now she bounces out of bed to be greeted by two hyper-active, over-excited, balls of boisterous energy. Although she'd love to let them on her bed, I remind her of the house rules. It might be cute now while they're small-ish, but when they're the size of a donkey and crushing your limbs, it might not be so much fun.

Thursday 13 September

The House Rules:

1. No dogs on the sofa
2. No dogs on beds
3. No feeding them human food
4. No feeding them from the table
5. No chewing furniture
6. No jumping up
7. No barking in the garden

Friday 14 September

It's the pups' first check-up and weigh-in at the vets. Getting them into their harnesses is nothing short of a comedy skit. I imagine trying to get a docile puppy into a harness for the first time would be hard enough, but trying to get two over-excited puppies into harnesses with zero intention of them being any help is practically impossible. It would be easier sculpting jelly. Actually, it would be easier sculpting jelly whilst riding a unicycle and juggling fire, wearing a blindfold. What's needed is three people. Per puppy. The first to sedate the puppy, the second to figure out which way around the bloody thing goes and the third to lift each leg into the relevant loops. What should have taken a few minutes took fifteen minutes of both Ivan and me scrambling around trying to figure out which strap went where, whilst trying to hold one pup long enough to get a leg in without being head-butted by the other. So far, we have Otis's two front paws in the same leg loop whilst Kiara is spinning in circles and hurling her harness around like a dead rabbit.

We gave up and squeezed them into the cat carrier but arrived too late and missed our appointment slot.

Monday 17 September

The pups' adventures into the big wide world are coming ever closer as they are getting their first vaccination today. As exciting as this was for the family, I didn't think it warranted a day off school. Also, I had to rush out to get Ivan a present for his birthday tomorrow. Although I'm a natural multi-tasker, I thought perhaps carrying two heavy, wriggling puppies across a main road into the vets probably wasn't the wisest or safest thing to do.

I picked up Otis first, who collapsed into my arms like a giant sack of potatoes, and plonked him on the vet's table while I went back for Kiara. Kiara had other ideas and had wedged herself underneath the passenger seat with the intention of going nowhere. I couldn't pull her out for love nor money and had to get into the back seat, coax her onto my lap and then wriggle my way out of the car with her still sitting on me so she didn't realise she was actually leaving the car. It looked ridiculous, but it worked, and I got her into the vets before she knew what hit her.

Lovely Penny, who'd always been so kind to me when we lost our cats, was absolutely thrilled to meet them both and made lots of fuss. Keen for them to associate going to the vets as a positive experience, she got out the treat jar. Otis scoffed as many treats as he could get his paws on, almost taking Penny's fingers with them. But Kiara refused and watched cautiously, eyeing Penny as if she was some kind of secret agent tricking her into taking cyanide. It was going to take more work than a few treats to win Kiara over. They weighed a whopping 10.7 and 9.7 kilos and we'd only had them a week. I wondered whether this growth speed was normal.

Tuesday 18 September – Ivan's Birthday

Ivan was very pleased with his birthday present which was a case of wine from me and some gardening vouchers from the pups, which after destroying his tropical Gunnera plant, was the least they could do. Ella had made him a lovely card and painted him a picture of our new family, including both pups and all three of our haloed cats. The pups were almost the same size as us in the painting which I thought was probably going to be true to scale before long.

We ordered a takeaway as it was too early to leave the pups by themselves. We had four beady eyes watching every mouthful we ate and drooling at every crunch of a poppadum. But sticking to the House Rules, we didn't cave in and give them any food. As tempting as those pleading doe-eyes were, we held strong.

We sat on the sofa to watch a movie, but with both pups constantly trying to jump on to join us, I ended up sitting on the floor with them both fighting over my lap. Kiara won – naturally – and curled up and went to sleep. She was already too big to fit on my lap and both her back legs dangled on the floor. Otis lay next to me with his head on my knee. He tried to inch his way on further, but Kiara nudged her way over every time he tried – the little minx. My bum was numb, my legs went dead and my knees were soggy with dog dribble. As Ivan and Ella giggled away at the movie on our comfortable sofa and the pups snored softly, I thought perhaps it was a good idea to buy the pups a sofa of their own.

Wednesday 19 September

Got up super early to exercise the pups in the garden before going to the school charity coffee morning. The plan is for the pups to sleep while I'm out so I don't return to a Home Alone situation. It's a gorgeous sunny morning, so I run into the garden with them before the builders arrive. They switch into manic mode and chase each other until they are panting and out of breath, then collapse on the lawn. Job done! I feed them and put them to bed, then drop Ella at school and attend the event. I look like I've been dragged through a hedge backwards as I didn't have time to brush my hair or do my makeup, but when I tell people I have two Ridgeback puppies, their faces say it all. I stuff my face with pastries since I skipped breakfast, which reminds me that I must do a food shop. The kitchen cupboards are looking pretty bare lately. The laundry room, however, is bulging with food. Dog food. Every kind of food and flavour imaginable. There's no room for washing in there now that I have two hungry dogs to feed and treat. Talking of treats, who knew there were so many different types of treats for pets these days. From cheap junk treats made of the entrails of god knows what to ludicrously expensive healthy treats with pumpkin, squash, vitamins and minerals which clean their teeth, gloss their coats and keep them regular. I'm not sure which dogs actually eat these healthy treats. When I offered Otis a healthy, over-priced biscuit made of spirulina and charcoal, he gagged, dropped it on the floor and looked at me like WTF is that! The junk treats, however, he gobbles down whole. Generally speaking, the healthier the treat, the less they like it. Dog treats may have moved on from the old days of Bonio and rawhide, but the taste buds haven't. Just like kids, give 'em junk and they'll love it! So, with four feeds a day of top-notch quality food I think I'll stick to the cheap treats for now so I have some money left over to feed the human family.

Thursday 20 September

Ella's twin friends came over for tea after school. Excitement to meet the pups rapidly turned into terror at the sheer size of them. I suppose when you're eight years old, two wild ponies charging towards you at full speed is quite alarming. I'm teaching the pups not to jump up and terrify other people's precious children, but the lure of a kid's dinner is just too much for them. They jump gazelle-like straight onto the dining table and scoff down both meals, leaving the kids screaming and running for their lives.

New house rule: #8 – Do not allow dogs to feed from the table or *on* the table.

Friday 21 September

Getting two puppies whilst having a kitchen extension built, in hindsight, probably wasn't the best idea. Advantages include: getting dogs used to ear-piercing drills, loud banging, multiple strange men around the house at the crack of dawn along with shouting, swearing, smoking and drinking vodka at 8 a.m. in the morning (them, not me). Disadvantages, however, include: front door being left wide open onto busy road, heavy objects being randomly dropped from the roof without warning, noxious products being left open and dangerous equipment being left around, such as saws and blades. All things I'd have trouble explaining to the pet insurance company should anything unfortunate happen.

Note to builders: Please do not leave your cigarette butts on the patio as pups think these are delicious dog treats. Thank you.

Saturday 22 September

Ivan was first up and I was basking in the delight of my first lie-in since getting the pups. That was until I heard a bloodcurdling yowl coming from the garden. I leapt out of bed and saw Ivan with his hand at Otis's bum, trying to pull something out of it. There was a look between horror and astonishment on Ella's face as Ivan pulled out, as if by magic, what looked like a collar with its buckle still attached! Otis's missing white collar! I was completely gobsmacked, not only that he'd managed to eat his own collar whole, but that it had taken this long to come out! Dogs have died from less! These dogs are clearly robust. Once the collar was fully extracted and Otis had stopped wailing, he went back to playing with Kiara as if nothing had happened. The three of us just looked at the collar hanging from Ivan's fingers with amazement.

'It's not white anymore,' Ella said.

At least we know we've got the right dog.

Monday 24 September

Half-dressed and barely awake, I open my curtains and spot the vodka-swilling builder chasing Kiara around the garden. She has something white hanging from her mouth, and by the panicked look on the builder's face, I guessed it was one of his cloths doused in toxic chemicals which he'd left lying around. I rushed out to join the chase which Kiara thought was great fun at 7 o'clock in the morning. As we both ran around after her like characters from a Benny Hill sketch, he mumbled something to me in Polish which I assumed meant, don't worry I've got this, as he lunged at her and grabbed her by the collar. I caught up and realised with horror that the thing in her mouth was not a builder's rag but a used sanitary towel she'd taken out of my bin! In blind panic, I snatched it out of her mouth and stuffed it into my dressing gown pocket, praying that he hadn't seen what it was. I spluttered words along the lines of, 'Everything is fine,' as I marched back into the house, scarlet with embarrassment. I glanced up at the roof and the entire crew of Polish builders were watching and sniggering. The poor vodka man shouted some kind of apology after me as I collapsed onto my bed, sweaty and humiliated, and in serious need of a stiff drink. I wonder if he has any vodka left.

Tuesday 25 September

Niggled by the puppies' rapid weight gain, I Googled the growth speed of large dogs and apparently, all is normal, so nothing to worry about. Reading on, I discover that Rhodesian Ridgebacks aren't fully grown until they are... two years old! Which means at this speed they'll be 100 stone! Oh, hang on, the growth rate dramatically slows down at nine months. That's a relief, just 50 stone then.

Just to triple check, I went on the Facebook puppy page which E had set up for us all when we got the puppies. Otis is by far the biggest. I do further research across various sites about size and feeding, and discover that it's important that your puppy doesn't grow too quickly or they'll have bone problems later. I'm following the feeding guidelines but decide to cut down on the portion size of their four feeds a day for now, just to be safe.

Wednesday 26 September

Ella has her school photo this morning and looks very smart in her new winter uniform. Nothing like a freshly ironed crisp white shirt. Otis didn't feel the same way and slapped two great muddy paw prints onto it by jumping up just as we were leaving the house (House Rule #6 re jumping up needs work). I told Ella to button up her cardigan and no one would notice, but as she pointed out, it was an Indian summer and she'd probably collapse from heatstroke, so I promised to drop in a freshly ironed shirt before the photos. I managed to do it just in time, by the skin of my teeth.

On the way home, I took a risk and squeezed in a quick food shop, half expecting the living room to be destroyed when I got home, but to my astonishment, the puppies were fast asleep and the room was completely intact. They rushed up to the baby gate when they heard me and I gave them a big cuddle.

'Good puppies,' I told them. I nipped to the loo and when I returned, my heart stopped. My beautiful hot-pink velvet chair had been completely stripped of its fabric and the seat entirely unstuffed, in less than the time it took me to do a wee! It was almost impressive what they could do in three minutes. I couldn't be totally sure who the culprit was, but since Otis copies everything Kiara does, and the chair was destroyed in record time, I was pretty sure it was a joint effort.

'That's NAUGHTY!' I said, but as neither pup was anywhere near the carnage at this point they had no idea what I was angry about so there was little else I could do other than weep.

Friday 28 September – My Birthday!

The builders were here at their usual ungodly hour, laughing and hacking up last night's fags while telling jokes in Polish and generally getting in the way.

I spent the morning washing the pups' bedding, wee-soaked towels and clearing up unidentifiable objects which were chewed BAR – Beyond All Recognition. I rushed to Ella's music assembly and made it just in time to hear her solo, then had a lovely lunch at The Ivy with girlfriends. I couldn't help but continually check my watch as I didn't want to leave the pups in their crates longer than two hours. I've decided after Chair-gate, that they need to be contained whilst I'm out both for their own safety and if we'd like our existing furniture to remain fit for purpose.

I popped into the pet store on the way home and bought the pups some rawhide-free chews. Apparently, rawhide is toxic so all the stuff we gave our dogs in the 80s should have killed them multiple times. Maybe dogs also have nine lives.

It was a blessed relief to come home and see the builders had left early. It's funny how Fridays are still a half day when the deadline is overdue, but today I was grateful.

When I opened the front door, the baby gate was open. I walked into the kitchen and saw what looked like a puppy foam party but was in fact my two new birthday cushions completely unstuffed and splayed all over the floor. There wasn't an inch of floor space not covered in the stuff. There, sat Otis, floating on a cloud of fluff, looking as guilty as sin as 100 quid's worth of cushions were decimated. Kiara looked as pleased as punch with herself as she rolled around to her heart's content, legs flailing in the air.

The builders must have let them out and so the pups had decided to have a party on my birthday without me. Luckily, the new furry beanbag Ella had bought me was safely locked away in my bedroom. I don't even want to think about the carnage that would have caused with a million tiny polystyrene balls.

Saturday 29 September

The pups are having their second vaccination today which means I can release the beasts into the wild (well, Surrey countryside) in a week's time. I'm not sure how the world is going to cope with these two, but I'm hoping more stimulation will calm them down a bit.

We have to see a locum as lovely Penny isn't in today. The moment Otis sees him he makes a run for the door, but the locum grabs him by the harness and picks him up off the floor with all four feet dangling. Otis looks at me and I grimace. Kiara just waits and watches, wide-eyed, plotting her revenge no doubt. He plonks Otis on the table and checks him over. Otis's back legs are shaking.

'He's a bit of a wimp, isn't he?' he snorts.

'Not usually,' I say protectively.

The locum gets out what looks like a Nerf gun and stabs him in the neck with it.

'Next!' he laughs.

But no one is laughing. Certainly not Otis and neither is Kiara. She looks at me, eyes black with fear.

'Can you just do Kiara's injection with her on the floor please? She's quite anxious.'

'Well, they say dogs are like their owners.'

Who is this arsehole? I fight the urge to slap him, and instead I say, 'Penny usually gives them a treat to reinforce a *positive* association with coming here.'

'Really?' he smirks. 'I don't like to buy dogs' affection with treats. I like to earn it.'

I almost burst out laughing and asked, how's that going for you? But I bit my tongue and made a hasty retreat. Just as we were halfway out the door he said to me,

'You know your male dog is going to be over 50 kilos when he's fully grown? You'd better learn how to control him or it'll be dangerous.' I steady myself and say to him that this isn't the case as their mother and father were only 35 and 38 kilos.

'Did you meet the father?' he asks.

'No,' I reply.

'That's because they didn't want you to know how big he was,' he finished arrogantly.

He swung the door, it clicked shut and I gave him the finger. The receptionist pretended not to notice, but I saw her smile. I paid the bill and looked down at my two giant terrified puppies. Uncontrollable? Dangerous? Please, who does this idiot think he is.

CHAPTER 3 – OCTOBER

TWIN TRAINING – THE WORST OF BOTH WORLDS

Age: 3 months
Weight: Otis 17.6 kg / Kiara 14.5 kg

Monday 1 October — Pups first training session

Today is our first session with experienced dog trainer, Steve. Steve is not the sort of guy to sugar-coat anything and has already told me, in no uncertain terms, to give one of the dogs back, before it's too late. Discovering I hadn't followed his sound advice, he was still willing to give it a go using his tried and tested techniques in training large dogs over the past twenty years.

To say I'm pinning all my hopes on him being able to train these two is an understatement. I'm actually considering changing my will and leaving him everything I own if he makes any progress today.

When I open the door, even I'm scared of Steve. He is a cross between a market trader and an aging skinhead. I wasn't sure whether this was a good thing or a bad thing, but looking at the dogs who'd scarpered at the sight of him, I figured it wasn't good. Steve shook my hand with a crushing handshake and informed us that he was training *us* and not the dogs. He said that first he wanted to demonstrate something with us.

'Can ya speak Japanese?' he asked Ivan.

'Er, no.' Ivan looked puzzled.

Steve then started shouting at Ivan in Japanese and pushed him down by his shoulders so that Ivan was sitting on the sofa.

'D'you understand that?' Steve asked.

'No.' Was this guy out of his mind?

Then Steve repeated it and pushed Ivan onto the sofa again.

'How 'bout now?'

'No.' Ivan did not look pleased.

Then Steve gently pushed Ivan into the sitting position and said softly, 'Suwatte kudasai.'

He told Ivan to stand up then did it again, repeating, 'Suwatte kudasai'.

Ivan sat obediently like a good boy.

'What d' you think suwatte kudasai means?'

The penny dropped. 'It means, sit down,' Ivan said.

''Zactly. When you talk to your dog without demonstrating 'zactly what it means, they'll 'ave no clue what you're asking 'em to do.' Steve beamed. 'One or two simple words along wiv the action, repeated until they understand, is the only way to successfully train a dog.'

It made complete sense. Except that he didn't have one dog to train, he had two dogs, in tandem. Plus, they were both mad.

'Right then, let's teach these dogs 'ow to 'eel,' Steve said confidently.

As I'd already informed Steve that I'd taught the pups basic words like sit, lie and paw, etc., I presumed he'd chosen this advanced instruction to "heel", so that I didn't get dragged under a bus on our first walk in the outside world. I could see that his methods were firm but fair and I loved him for it. The dogs hated him for it. Otis was hiding in the curtains and Kiara was lodged under the printer table. Steve said he wanted them in their harnesses for the training session as their necks were too tender for collars at twelve weeks. It took an embarrassing ten minutes for Ivan to dislodge Kiara from under the table, and for me to get Otis out of the curtains and get the bloody things on.

I'd read that wearing a harness for some breeds encourages them to pull, like a Husky. For Otis and Kiara, it was like putting a twin-turbo supercharger on them. They pulled me down the garden with such force, I thought my arms had come out of their sockets. When Steve caught up, Kiara veered off to the right and hid under a tree, and Otis leapt into my arms, knocking me flying. I dusted myself off and handed Otis to Steve whilst I took hold of Kiara. You'd think Steve was taking them to slaughter the way they behaved around him. I told them both to calm down, which was about as effective as telling a toddler, mid-tantrum, to chill out.

'I'll demonstrate wiv Otis then you copy wiv Kiara,' Steve said.

Steve then held a tasty treat by his side and confidently said, 'heel' presumably to entice Otis to stand next to him, thereby learning the word. Instead, Otis turned to me and sprung into my arms again, hurtling Steve into the air then flat on his face. Otis ran down the garden back into the kitchen, followed by Kiara. I was mortified.

'I fink the problem is they don't trust me yet,' Steve said, brushing the weeds off his tummy. That's putting it mildly, I thought.

'As the session is almost up, why don't we leave it 'ere for today and then next time they see me, they'll know who I am.' That's what I was worried about.

'Don't worry, luv, we'll get there,' he assured me.

I loved his optimism but had a feeling these "tried and tested techniques" may need some serious tweaking with these two.

Tuesday 2 October

Prior to getting the pups, I'd arranged a girl's day out in London and actually laughed out loud at my ludicrous expectation of being able to leave these two by themselves for an entire day. Instead, I spent the day teaching the pups new words to add to their expanding repertoire. I didn't bother with "heel" after yesterday's experience, choosing simpler words such as "drop it" and "leave it" which I thought would still be incredibly useful given their penchant to grab and run off with anything that wasn't nailed down including bras, socks, magazines, remote controls, shoes, oven gloves and DVDs.

There's no doubt Ridgebacks are an intelligent breed, but teaching them together makes them look like they share a single brain cell between them. They cannot concentrate for a second when they are together and any attempt at training swiftly turns into a rugby scrum. I thought shutting one out of the room while I teach the other would work, but this is torture for them as dogs suffer from FOMO (fear of missing out) more than humans. The one shut away makes such a racket trying to get to us that I can't even hear myself think. I have to ask Ella to entertain the one not being trained just to give me five minutes before the trainee realises the other one is having more fun and breaks free. It is frustrating but I have to say, even in five minutes, they can learn a fair amount. Otis is a lot faster at learning than Kiara. So much for him being the dope.

Dogs repertoire so far:

Sit
Paw

Off
Down
Outside
Wee wee
Wait
Ready, steady, GO
Ball
Bed
Stop that or I'm sending you back (okay, not this one)
Treat – definitely their favourite word (and mine)

When I talk to Otis, he cocks his head from side to side and his ears move backwards and forwards like antennae tuning in. His face is so expressive, like he's trying hard to understand what I'm saying. Kiara looks at me deadpan, without expression. While Otis follows an instruction, regardless of whether there's a treat incentive or not, Kiara won't do anything unless it's worth her while. She will only make the effort if it's a high-value treat like a piece of fish or chicken. If it's a Rich Tea biscuit, you can forget it.

Wednesday 3 October

Being a good dog parent takes up a lot of time, a heck of a lot more than I was anticipating. As well as the feeding, the training, the exercising and the playing, there's the supervising to keep them and your worldly goods safe from harm. Whilst other puppy parents tell me that their pups sleep for most of the day, mine barely sleep for thirty minutes in a twelve-hour period, which means on average I'm getting about five minutes of work done a day and the washing basket is taller than the Eiffel Tower.

So, I've decided to get the pups into a Gina Ford-style baby routine so that hopefully I'll get around three hours of work done while Ella's at school, and maybe even a few chores.

The Puppy Plan is as follows:

6.30	Get pups up and play in garden
7.00	Pups' breakfast (meal 1)
8.00	Take Ella to school
9.00	Train pups (recall, heel, stay etc. – the serious stuff)
10.00	Mid-morning feed (meal 2)
10.30	Pups sleep for two hours while I work
1.00	Pups' lunch (meal 3)
1.30	Walk/Play with pups
2.30	Pups sleep while I work
3.30	Collect Ella
6.00	Pups' dinner (meal 4) and feed human family
7.00	Pups in bed so I can get on with chores and spend time with family

Results:

Pups didn't sleep for a second during the entire day. The moment one falls asleep, the other one wakes them up and they play, fight and get up to no good.

Still, Rome wasn't built in a day. Tomorrow is another day.

Thursday 4 October

Time puppies spent sleeping = 0
Hours I spent working = 0
Likelihood of being fired = 100%
Which would be awkward given that my husband is my boss.

Friday 5 October

I've cracked it! In order for the pups to sleep, I have to separate them. Why on earth didn't I think of this sooner? Ridiculously, I thought they weren't tired but they are exhausted. They're only hyperactive because they're winding each other up and getting overtired. At 10 a.m. on the dot, I put them in their separate crates and they were out for the count the moment their heads hit the pillow. They slept until 1.00 p.m. which meant I could get three hours of work done. Instead, I watched three hours of daytime television, but that was to celebrate the breakthrough. I'll start the proper version of the routine on Monday.

Am now regretting that I signed up to ballet classes on a Friday night. The idea was to do something calming whilst toning my body, but all I want to do at the end of the day is collapse onto a (dog-free) sofa with a G&T and not squeeze something else into my packed day. I'm definitely burning enough calories just chasing after the dogs but Ella is chuffed to bits to be dog-sitting while Ivan watches the footie upstairs, so I force myself to go.

Apparently, the pups were as good as gold while I was out, and Ella played with them until they fell asleep. "They" being all three of them who were fast asleep on the sofa when I got in. House rule #1 broken in style.

Saturday 6 October – Puppy Play

We were all excited about the puppies' first play session at our local pet shop. It's basically a few hours in a sectioned-off area where a group of puppies can play and socialise together for free every Saturday morning. According to other owners, the puppies absolutely love it and it's great for getting them used to other dogs early on, to prevent problems like anxiety and aggression. Ivan loved the idea of something for free.

We decided to go to this bonding experience together as a family, and I'd arranged with a mum from school who'd just got a puppy, to meet us there. Otis and Kiara were so nervous that we spent the first ten minutes dragging them out of hiding places so they could play with the gorgeous little British Bulldog, Bruce, who was the only puppy who'd arrived so far. My two were twice the size of him and were absolutely terrified of him. Kiara tried frantically to get as far away from Bruce as possible by clambering up the shelving units on the wall, knocking off tins of pet food as she did, and then catapulted herself over the fence which was designed to keep her in. Every time we brought her back into the area, she did it again. And Otis copied her. After the fourth time of doing this, and apologising to shoppers and the patient dog owner, who was obviously hoping to socialise his well-behaved puppy, not teach him bad behaviour, they both wedged themselves so far under the shelving unit that I couldn't get them out. As Ella played happily with Bruce, and Ivan shook his head in exasperation, and shoppers looked on sympathetically, I used a broom handle to push them out the other side then grabbed them both by their collars and dragged them back to the car. One of the shop assistants called after me saying that they just needed to get used to it and assured me they'd be better next time. Next time? Nothing like blind optimism.

My phone pinged and a message from the mum at school apologising that she couldn't make it came through. In all the mayhem, I'd forgotten she was coming and felt a huge sigh of relief that she wasn't there to witness the havoc.

Sunday 7 October

Now the puppies are fully vaccinated, they are no longer confined to the garden and can go out for walks. I'd found a place called Circular Park which had been specifically designed with a fence all the way around to prevent dogs from running away. I thought this was a good place for our first family walk as the pups could be let off lead without fear of escaping. Unfortunately, half of Surrey had the same idea and it was heaving when we arrived.

As the parking area was already full (which seemed ridiculously early for a Sunday), we had to park on the road. Stupidly, we'd only brought the extra-long 10-metre leads with us and hadn't even made it to the park gate before all five of us were completely tangled up in them. We had to shuffle our way into the park and open the lead-heavy gates before detangling ourselves like a bunch of total amateurs.

Most of the dogs were miniature designer dogs and Otis and Kiara dwarfed them. I was getting quite a few looks from owners which I interpreted as, *why are you bringing two ponies into our quiet little park*. It wasn't helped by the fact that Kiara had gone into full manic mode and was chasing every dog she laid her eyes on. Getting her back was impossible, with her recall currently 0%. This isn't to say that she doesn't come back to us or that she doesn't know her name. It just means she comes back in her own good time and not when we call her. I couldn't assess Otis's recall as he didn't leave my side the entire time. He spent most of the time scrambling up my legs trying to be carried. By the end of the walk, most of the other owners were carrying their dogs just to keep them away from Kiara.

On our way out, we bumped into an old friend whose dogs were as crazy as mine. On the one hand, it made me feel better knowing we weren't the only lepers in the park, but on the other hand it horrified me. If she can't train two small dogs in eighteen months, then what chance do I have!

Monday 8 October

My brother accidentally cut his finger off on the machinery at work and I needed to drive him into London to see the surgeon. Having to explain to Ivan that he is going to have to look after the pups for an unspecified amount of time (who knows how long we'll be waiting) was a more delicate matter than whether my brother could have his finger sewn back on or not.

Although not on my list of top ten days out, watching my brother have a series of painful injections in his hand and a rather patronising but handsome surgeon giving us his medical opinion, was still preferable to looking after two mad puppies for a day.

Wednesday 10 October

Getting the pups into a routine is a godsend, giving me a few hours of peace while they sleep. However, the rest of the time I am watching them like a hawk as getting into mischief is their favourite activity of the day. Kiara chews everything other than her chew toys, including piano legs, chair legs, sofa corners and skirting boards. When I catch her, I tell her firmly 'no' and she looks at me and goes back to chewing. I distract her with other toys but she is far more interested in destroying furniture than playing with dog toys. I have sprayed the corners of the furniture with some foul-smelling repellent which is supposed to put them off chewing it, but Kiara just waits for me to finish then starts chewing the exact spot I've just sprayed. Working in the garden office is preferable as there's less to chew in there, although she did manage to destroy two laptop cables today with her razor-sharp puppy teeth and then finish off my set of new folders which were under the desk.

Saturday 13 October – Puppy Play Part 2

Not being a family of quitters, we decided a second attempt at Puppy Play was worth a try. This time, the pups knew what was coming and were having none of it, but I was one step ahead of them. As they bolted to their hiding spot, I beat them to it and blocked the underneath of the shelving unit with a dog bed. Victory only lasted a second when a Chihuahua puppy called Vivienne, who was the size of a snack, came scurrying in and sent the pups into a complete frenzy. Fearing what Kiara might do, I thought it best for all involved if we left immediately before another incident occurred. But Kiara had other plans and managed to leap on top of the shelving unit, followed by Otis, and the weight of them together toppled the entire unit onto its side along with all the dog beds. Both pups then jumped over the gate and ran towards the shop exit towards the car park. By the love of God, my friend Jane came into the shop just as they reached the door, and both pups, thinking she had come to rescue them, made a run for her instead.

'Grab them!' I shouted. She got them by their collars and once again I marched them back to the car. The young shop assistant avoided eye contact this time as I apologised for the mayhem we'd caused yet again. I assured her not to worry, we would not be back next weekend or any other weekend for that matter. The look on her face was one of sheer relief. I'll have to brainstorm another way to get them socialising with other puppies.

Sunday 14 October

The pups' mum, Jasmine, and one of their siblings are coming to visit today. I'd read that Ridgebacks enjoyed their own kind more than the company of other breeds and thought this might be a good way to socialise them without them trying to escape or wrecking the joint.

When they turned up, they had a second puppy from the litter with them which they were looking after. Five Ridgebacks in our house was quite a sight. I was struck by how much they all looked alike and how stunning they were, but mainly I was taken aback by the sheer size of Jasmine who dwarfed her puppies. I'd put fleeces on the sofa in case any of the dogs decided to jump on it, and Jasmine read this as her cue to make herself right at home. Otis observed her taking up half the sofa, and climbed on to join her. I didn't have the heart to tell him to get off as he waddled over to the opposite end, unnerved by the size of this dog in his house.

Neither Otis nor Kiara showed any signs of recognition of their mother or their siblings which I found strange considering they'd only been apart for a month. Otis was dubious about having other dogs in the house, but his curiosity got the better of him and after checking out each pup, he joined in playing with them. Kiara was nowhere to be seen.

We went into the garden and Ivan threw a ball for Jasmine who looked more like a deer than a dog. The speed at which she ran for the ball and the pounding of her feet on the ground was startling. Ivan and I exchanged glances and knew exactly what the other was thinking. We are going to have TWO of these giant beasts. As the puppies ran around together, Ella was in complete bliss. All the toys – which had been ignored up to this point – were finally getting broken-in and they were all having a blast. Except Kiara. I knew E had a soft spot for Kiara and I went to find her so she could have a cuddle before she left. I found her hiding in the living room curtains. She'd wrapped herself up so tightly in them so she couldn't be spotted. I picked her up gently and handed her to E who was thrilled to see her. But Kiara was unsettled. E put her down just long enough for me to snap a quick photo of the puppies all together before Kiara ran back indoors. She didn't come out again until they'd all gone home.

Monday 15 October

Third weigh-in at the vets. They nearly broke the scales. Going for the Guinness Book of Records, I fear.

Wednesday 17 October

Breaking news… the extension is FINALLY FINISHED! When I say finished, I mean the builders have officially left and moved onto another job. We still have no cupboard doors, radiators or taps, minor things I'm willing to overlook for the sake of my sanity and the puppies' welfare. I'm sure Ella's lovely paintings from school can be stuck over the holes which the builders left in the walls. The ceiling hole might be a bit trickier.

Thursday 18 October

We spent the morning moving the pups into the new kitchen extension. It must be the most expensive dog pen ever built. The original plan was to give us a separate living area, but the large space and access straight onto the patio and into the garden makes it an ideal place to house the dogs while they're still puppies. There are also limited items to chew – other than a piano (which now has bubble-wrapped feet). Ivan thinks the crate fleeces look ugly as they don't match the pink and teal colour scheme, and suggests I make some matching covers for their crates. As this is about as far down my priority list as is possible, I should get these done by their fifth birthday.

Friday 19 October

As well as wearing suitable clothing and colours when looking after two puppies (pastels are a distant memory), jewellery can also pose a problem. Unless you're planning to make your necklace into two bracelets, nothing longer than a choker can be worn. One swipe of a paw when jumping up and it's history for that lovely chain. Same with hoop earrings. Unless you want four ear lobes, studs are the only safe option.

Saturday 20 October

We are taking the pups for their first social outing to a new dog café for brunch. Ella was excited by the novelty of a café for dogs, and Ivan had been enticed by the prospect of a big veggie fry-up.

With larger harnesses fitted, we actually got the pups into the car and wearing seatbelts for the first time, which was an achievement in itself (and a legal requirement). The café had no parking anywhere near it so we had to park on the main road and prevent two enthusiastic puppies, darting all over the place, from getting run over. Fortunately, we remembered the short leads today.

Walking the puppies separately is difficult but just about doable. Obviously, at twelve weeks, they can't yet walk to "heel" and instead pull on the lead whilst criss-crossing in front of you. Without notice, they will stop dead in their tracks to smell something, hurtle forwards again, then dart backwards to smell something they must have missed on the way but somehow can detect now they've passed it. As the walker (or walkee in this case), you are literally being yanked backwards and forwards like a yoyo. When you add in passers-by, other dogs and loud traffic noises to the mix, there really isn't a moment where you can afford to lose your concentration. But as I say, it's just about doable.

However, when there are two of them together, it's a death wish. They will not walk next to each other or behind each other. They both want to be in front and so tug on the lead to overtake the other one. Every time Kiara stops or reacts to anything, Otis shoves her out of the way to take a look. They criss-cross paths continually and tangle their leads so Ivan and I have to keep swapping places or exchanging dogs so they don't become a tangled mess. They have no road sense whatsoever and would happily dart into the road to sniff a week-old bird poo rather than live another day. It takes all our strength, concentration and patience just to walk them down the road to the café. When Ella asks if she can walk one, I almost bite her head off. I want to enjoy a family breakfast, not sit in A&E for the day with a daughter and a dislocated shoulder or worse. Fortunately, we all make it to the café in one piece and in need of a hearty breakfast.

Dog cafes are bizarre places. People of all ages from all walks of life, sitting at tables having breakfast with their dogs, some on their laps and others sitting on their own chair, quite frankly, looks weird. I half expected one of the dogs to ask someone to pass the salt and sprinkle it on their eggs. I can't tell who's loving it more – the dogs or the owners. I'd never seen so many different breeds of dogs in one place, but we now have an immense knowledge of different breeds from playing Dog Bingo, and Ella identifies every single one from an Airedale Terrier to a Weimaraner.

We were shown to our table and given two menus – one for us and one for the dogs. Needless to say, we were the only family with two puppies and the only ones with Ridgebacks. They caused quite a stir. It would have been lovely to introduce them had they not resided under the table for the entire duration with Otis lying on top of Kiara. They did come out for their Puppacinos and their duffins (dog muffins) before retreating back under the table and then puking the whole lot up as soon as we got home. The human food was pretty decent although Ella refused to eat anything as she said the whole café smelt like dogs. She did have a point.

Sunday 21 October

I have woken up feeling as sick as a dog. The pups are hyper so Ella has taken them into the garden to play while I do their breakfast. Having weaned them off dry food, they are now eating the recommended raw food which means I have to remember to defrost it the night before and be uber careful to wipe down every surface after each feed so there are no traces of bacteria to kill the human family. Raw dead animal is not the most pleasant thing to see first thing in the morning, particularly when you're vegan and feeling so unwell.

As they hurtle around the garden, I can smell an atrocious stench coming from the living room. My lilac-ombre curtains are brown. Otis comes running in, skids past me and squirts a gallon of diarrhoea horizontally across the curtains like a spray gun, which makes me want to hurl. I didn't know that shit could spray out horizontally until I saw it myself first-hand. The poor pup just stood there as the explosion happened, not knowing what to do. I stuck cotton wool up each nostril and soaked the curtains in buckets of soapy water. I spent the rest of the day cleaning up puddles of diarrhoea, and wiping down walls and cupboards which Otis involuntarily spray-gunned throughout the day. This was not the way I was hoping to spend my "sick day". Ivan left to watch the football down the pub, leaving me to deal with all the shit. Literally. I blame the dog café for all of this.

Monday 22 October

It's half term and the novelty of having two puppies means we are still in popular demand. Ella's cousins came over to meet the pups and have a play for the afternoon. Unbelievably, the pups were on their best behaviour, mainly because of all the attention and the fact that I was keeping a beady eye on them. I was pleased that other than a couple of knocked-over plant pots and a giant tear in the trampoline safety net, all four children left intact without any scratches, bruises or missing items of clothing.

A very successful day.

Tuesday 23 October

Getting up at the crack of dawn to let the pups outside for a wee, I don't mind. Playing with them for half an hour before it's barely light outside is not quite so much fun now it's getting colder. But they can't be trusted in the garden without supervision, which was proven last night. I'd left them alone outside while I went to the loo as I fancied weeing in peace without them fighting over the loo roll. When I returned to the garden, the giant rip in the trampoline safety net was now, no net at all. What was left of the remains was being used in a tug of war between them.

I consoled myself that the net did look ugly. We never had safety nets when we were kids and nothing bad happened. Maybe it would toughen kids up or make them more aware if there wasn't a net there for safety.

Wednesday 24 October

Our neighbours popped round this morning to bring their little boy to see the puppies. After stroking Otis and Kiara, they asked politely if they could meet the puppies.

'These *are* the puppies,' I said.

Their surprise was quickly terminated when their three-year-old was catapulted off the trampoline when Otis and Kiara jumped on to join him.

I may have to look into getting another safety net.

Thursday 25 October

A second trip to the hospital is needed for my brother to see what surgery is possible. I toy with the idea of taking both pups with me, then come to my senses. So, my options are:

A. leaving an eight-year-old child to dog-sit which is not sensible and probably illegal

B. locking them in the living room and coming back to Armageddon
C. leave a thank-you note for Ivan with a large bottle of whiskey, and leg it before he realises I've gone

I chose C.

Saturday 27 October

Ella needs a new pair of school shoes as the pups ate the last pair. Jane is free and happy to look after the pups for a couple of hours while we're out. I need to give the house a good clean before she arrives. It looks like a bomb's gone off – how can two animals create so much mess and dirt? I seem to have a broom, a mop or a hoover in my hand at any given hour of the day and it still looks like a shit heap. If I was being paid by the hour to clean, I'd be earning six figures by now.

I moved the sofa and found an entire shops-worth of toys and household objects. The pups seem totally uninterested in anything created by the design experts for the canine community. These designers would be far better off just selling lucky-dip packets containing used plasters, socks, lids and shoes. Maybe I should start my own line. I certainly have enough stock.

Wednesday 31 October
Steve's training session Part two

To prove we weren't a family of imbeciles, and to not waste half the lesson, we already had the pups in their harnesses before Steve arrived. I was determined for this training session to be a success.

We decided to train the pups separately today. Since Kiara is the alpha dog, Steve said we should start with her. She certainly looked like the alpha dog as she yanked Steve down the end of the garden then darted around, helter-skelter, tying Steve up in knots with her lead. After unravelling himself, he asked me to take Kiara's lead and follow his instructions.

Kiara refused to respond to any instruction, refused any form of treat – even the chopped sausage he'd brought with him – and just laid on the floor in total defiance. That was until the neighbour's dog was let into their garden, when she took part in a barking match of who could outlast the other. Undefeated and still full of grit, Steve suggested we swap dogs since Kiara is very sensitive outside (meaning she has the concentration span of a gnat).

I locked Kiara in the kitchen and took Otis outside. Otis seemed very willing to come out which was encouraging. Until Steve took hold of his lead. As soon as he did this, Otis sat down, ignored whatever Steve said and wouldn't budge. We were still on the patio at this point and hadn't even made it into the garden. I managed to jolly Otis down to the end of the garden, but with Kiara barking wildly and pounding the patio door to get out, Otis couldn't concentrate on anything other than getting back to his crazed sister. He whined and whimpered, pulling so hard to get to her that it was impossible for anyone to concentrate, let alone try a new training technique. The barking stopped and Kiara disappeared for a moment. Then she took a run up to the patio door and threw herself into the glass in a desperate attempt to break free and join us. Exasperated, I locked her in her crate for one last attempt to train Otis, but all he did was hammer at the patio door to join her.

Steve tugged Otis to face away from his sister and Otis bit him – not hard, but just enough to let Steve know that he wasn't going to play ball. Poor Steve had to concede that he'd done all he could for today and tactfully suggested training them individually in a park next time, where they couldn't see, smell or hear each other. This seemed like a sensible idea.

I phoned Steve to book another session. He told me there had been a death in the family. I have a feeling I won't be hearing from Steve again.

CHAPTER 4 – NOVEMBER

DOGGY DAY CARE DISASTER

Thursday 1 November

Walking the dogs together on lead is an absolute no go. They are so strong now that I swear if these dogs could swim, I could water-ski behind them.

Taking them to a park where they can run free is the only option until they can walk like they're not trying to win the 100-metre sprint. Our local park, although small, is perfect for them while they are young, plus I can park near the gate which means I'm only dragged along for a few feet. Optimistically, on the way, I grabbed a takeaway coffee which my coat and tracksuit bottoms enjoyed thoroughly.

I can only walk the pups for twenty minutes as the recommended time for exercising puppies is five minutes per month of age. Any more than this can damage their hip joints. Unfortunately, this information has not trickled down to the canine population so we, as responsible owners, have to ensure they adhere to it. A mum at school took her puppy for extended walks whilst trying to lose her baby weight and ended up with a £12K bill from the SuperVet to replace the poor dog's hip. She could have had liposuction for less. I vigilantly stick to the time limit whilst out but am a bit concerned that the crazed running around the garden is racking up daily miles equivalent to an ultra marathon. The vet has assured me that it's fine since they will know when they've had enough. He doesn't know my dogs.

It is joyful watching the pups chasing each other around the park, and as it's quiet today I can practise their "recall" training without any distractions. At home, although "heel" training seems like a pipe dream, the recall training is going surprisingly well, with Otis at least. Otis practically has this command nailed and almost always comes to me when I call his name now. Kiara, on the other hand, almost never does. I know ideally we should have this command sussed before we try it out on a walk, but I fear we may never leave the house if we waited for this to happen.

The measure of success for recall is to call your dog's name just once, loudly and firmly, and they come straight back to you, whatever they are doing and wherever you are. This means you have complete control over any situation should they, or another being, be in danger, like near a road, chasing another dog, etc. It's also useful if you ever want to leave the park before it gets dark instead of spending half the night trying to catch your dog.

A useful tip I've been given is to stand in the same spot when I call them and not move until they come back. This is supposed to teach them that the walk does not continue until they do what they're told by their pack leader. This might work for some dogs, but Kiara takes this as carte blanche to go mental and greet every person in the park, chase every squirrel up a tree, knock over a few toddlers and generally have a bloody good time, with no one trying to stop her. Otis, with his FOMO and boundless enthusiasm, always joins in. If I was to actually wait in the same spot, Christmas would have come and gone. However, what I have discovered is that they panic like mad when I'm out of sight. Being stranded in the park without their useless pack leader is more terrifying than having a party in the park. And this trick works every single time.

I duck behind a tree and call their names, and when they realise they can't actually see me, they search in a blind panic. When they find me, I shower them with masses of praise and cuddles so they know this is the reward for coming back to me. The hope is that eventually they will put two and two together and associate me calling them with masses of praise. Otherwise, I'm going to have to carry a tree around with me everywhere I go.

Friday 2 November

Following the advice of the vast number of dog-expert friends I didn't know I had before I got two dogs, I begin the search for a doggy day-care centre. Apparently, this is an absolute must if you want your dog to be properly socialised and not be a social outcast. Personally, I just want a day off where I don't have to keep watch 24/7 and could actually get some basic chores done, like having a bath.

On phoning around, I realise it's not going to be a cheap day off as it's a full day's rate, regardless of how many hours they stay – and sadly no discount for two dogs. Most places don't encourage viewing the facilities and prefer you not to drop the dogs off either. This means the puppies are collected by a complete stranger in the morning, bundled into the back of a van with a load of other dogs (a bit 101 Dalmatians) and then returned home at the end of the day, hopefully in one piece. If I'm not in, I can leave them a key and they can let them in. I could just give them my debit card and pin number and they could collect their payment on the way home too! I don't know about doggy day-care, it sounds more like dodgy day-care. I'm also not happy sending my pups somewhere I can't view before agreeing to a monthly commitment. I mean, what are they trying to hide? I will continue the search after the weekend.

In the meantime, I have booked the pups onto separate training classes at a location far enough away that no one will recognise me or the dogs. The Puppy Training Foundation Course is a six-week course for puppies under five months, for an hour a week for the next six weeks. Therefore, killing two birds with one stone by socialising them *and* training them at the same time.

Saturday 3 November

As I'm fed up of sitting on the floor with the pups and getting pins and needles when watching TV, I have made the executive decision to allow the pups on the sofa *by invitation only*. It's cheaper than buying them their own suite and it is kind of nice to cuddle up to them. However, they are only allowed on the sofa when we are sitting on it and *invite* them to join us by saying "paws on". It's not so much breaking the rule, as bending it. They have plenty of large cushions to sleep on around the living room and have recently taken ownership of my birthday beanbag, so I don't think this is an unreasonable request.

As Kiara rolls around on the sofa, delighted by being able to join me, I notice a red rash on her tummy. It looks quite inflamed but doesn't seem to be bothering her. I'll keep an eye on it.

Sunday 4 November

Making a rainbow cake whilst supervising two puppies and nursing a hangover was not the best idea for a Sunday morning. Ella's job is to make the fondant rainbow to go on top of the cake and Otis and Kiara's job is not to eat it. We are making sure that one person is in the kitchen at all times so that all elements of the cake-making process stay exactly where they should be, i.e., on the counter not the floor, ceiling, dog beds or in dog stomachs. Therefore, the cake cannot be left unsupervised for one second.

The cake is iced, the rainbow placed on top and the pixies dotted around. It looks so pretty and Ella is thrilled. Although the pups' noses are not quite at the level of the counters yet, it only takes them to jump up with their front legs to reach anything. So, everything on the counters is now either put away or pushed back as far as possible so it cannot be reached by the two opportunists. They will pinch literally anything, edible or otherwise. And they do not discriminate: whisks, spoons, scales, tubs of butter, cartons of juice, you name it. I have put the cake on the top shelf in the kitchen where the dogs would need a ladder to reach it. And the ladder is in the shed which is fastened with a padlock and a code even I don't know.

Monday 5 November

Before I get the pups up, I check the cake is still in one piece. I don't know how I thought the pups could unlock their crates, grab the ladder, nick the cake then lock themselves back in, but they are intelligent dogs so I thought I'd better check. Luckily, the cake is in one piece and I carefully bring it down out of the sun with Kiara watching my every move, saliva dripping from her chops.

Kiara's rash has spread to her chest and it's warm to the touch so I take her to the vets just to be safe. Penny thinks it might be an allergic reaction to something (other than good behaviour) and suggests running allergy tests. A rough quote sends my blood pressure through the roof, especially when she says they're not usually conclusive and probably won't be covered by insurance. A good old-fashioned dose of suck-it-and-see seems like a good idea to me.

I pick up some hypoallergenic washing liquid on the way home and throw all their bedding in the wash, along with the sofa covers, and put them on a hot wash in case something is irritating her. I strip the furry bean bag and wash the cover. Kiara gives the coverless beanbag a curious poke with her nose. Now just a transparent net of white polystyrene balls, I know exactly what Kiara is thinking and place it well out of reach of her big, beady eyes.

Tuesday 6 November

I wangled a visit to a doggy day care centre and saw immediately why viewings are actively discouraged. Convicts on Death Row have better lodgings. It was absolutely chucking it down when I arrived and I had to stand in the rain getting drenched while the woman made several attempts to unpadlock the main gate. As the mud squelched over my pink satin trainers (another great decision), I spotted the centre which was a muddy field with a few plastic toys, a shed and some dirty cages for them to sleep in while they "rest" in the afternoon. "We wash and dry them before we bring them home" was an outside hose and a giant blow heater. As desperate as I was for some respite, I wouldn't send my worst enemy here. I asked how many dogs they usually have on any given day, to which they replied, 'Sometimes one or two but sometimes none.' None? So much for them being socialised.

I squelched back to the car with the mud now at my ankles and wondered why anyone would need to padlock that gate, unless it was to keep the dogs from escaping and running home.

The search continues for day-care (and a new pair of trainers).

Wednesday 7 November – Ella's 9th Birthday

The living room is a winter wonderland of polystyrene balls. The floor, the sofa and the walls are covered in them. I was certain I'd shut my bedroom door, but one way or another, they'd got hold of the beanbag. Trying to scoop up thousands of tiny static polystyrene balls could be an Olympic sport. It is virtually impossible. They literally multiply while you're clearing up. The dogs are completely covered in them and look like two yetis. There's nothing they don't stick to. They're even stuck on Kiara's eyeballs!

I don't know how I manage to get them off the dogs, but I somehow do, and shut the pups in their crates, spending hours hoovering up the damn things. When I take out the hoover bag, they shoot out all over the floor. I still have to decorate the room and get all the food ready for Ella's tea party after school, and I am not happy at all. I've bought an enormous inflatable unicorn which the pups are terrified of. Every time they even think of doing anything naughty, I chase them with it and they shoot off and hide in their beds. If it didn't fill half the living room, I'd leave it up permanently.

After the party…

Ella had a great time with her friends. The kids loved playing with the pups and Kiara only licked the cake once, knocking off a single pixie which I quickly managed to remove from her mouth before she swallowed it (they weren't edible). My folks came over when the girls left and the pups fell asleep on their laps, exhausted. The carcass of the beanbag was chucked in the dustbin along with the leftovers. Both pups opened their eyes and licked their lips when the last pieces of cake were handed to my parents. They'd been waiting three long days for this cake.

'No human food,' I reminded them as my dad gave them a piece of his cake. Oh well, it's a special occasion. There are always exceptions to the rules.

Thursday 8 November
Kiara's First Puppy-Training Session

It's a good job I left early as I got completely lost trying to find the training centre which is a farm in the middle of absolutely nowhere. At least I knew for certain there would be no one who'd recognise me in a place as remote as this.

I park in the make-shift car park and see a group of excitable owners with their puppies in a paddock. Kiara, thinking she's going for a walk, leaps out of the car with excitement, takes one look at the other puppies and leaps straight into the back seat. I drag her over to the paddock and she looks completely out of place. She's enormous compared to the other puppies, which isn't helped by the fact that the current trend is for Cockapoos and Dachshunds. I'm asked countless times how old she is just in case I've wandered into the wrong class with my overgrown puppy like an idiot. I'm making a badge for her for next week with her age on it, like the one Ella had on her birthday card.

Most people have never seen a Ridgeback before and are fascinated by her ridge. Fortunately, they don't try to touch it, possibly because she's wedged in between my legs in fear. As more puppies arrive, they greet each other with the obligatory bum sniff. Kiara, however, took her bum as far away from any puppy's nose as was possible. I tried to encourage some sniffing but she wasn't having any of it and sat down in case any pup had the audacity to even think about getting near her behind. Trying to be as friendly as I could with an overgrown puppy wedged between my legs wasn't easy. A jolly middle-aged lady with what looked like a guinea pig but was actually a miniature Dachshund puppy called Titan (seriously), made a beeline for me.

'Are you the lady with two Ridgebacks?' she asked. Oh god.

'Have you seen me walking them?' I asked innocently.

'No, my friend has seen you walk them in the park.'

"Walk" is a stretch and I don't wait for her to continue, instead I scurry off pretending Kiara needs a wee. What are the chances? I've deliberately trekked to the middle of bloody nowhere, and the dogs have only been out of the house a handful of times, and still I'm recognised.

Sharon, our trainer, took an instant dislike to me. She was a humourless, know-it-all who did not find any of my witty comebacks even the slightest bit amusing. Fortunately, the rest of my audience did, but this made her dislike me even more. She did not like Kiara, either, and the feeling was definitely mutual. Kiara might be a pain in the arse a lot of the time, but she has the instincts of a spiritual guru when it comes to sussing out someone's nature. It's her super power. There is no middle ground with Kiara. She either loves you or hates you and nothing you can do will change her mind. This was going to be one hell of a long hour for both of us.

Today the puppies were going to learn their marker word (good or yes), a loaded sit (no idea why it's loaded) and their name. Their name! These puppies are four months old, for goodness' sake. I wondered what the heck these owners had been doing all these weeks if their pups didn't know their names already. Kiara had been told off so many times she probably thought her name was Kiara No.

Sharon only had one volume level which was shouty. It was also nasally, and it was already starting to grate on me. She gave a patronising introduction to us dummies and got all the dogs onto their paws for their first exercise. I was told off for not bringing "high-value treats". In other words, something Kiara had never had before and would find irresistible. But this dog had nicked every food stuff known to man – there was literally nothing she hadn't tried. Sharon pressed some form of squished, sweaty meat cubes into my hand a little too pointedly.

'This should do it,' she said and waved the treats in front of Kiara, expecting her to hang on her every word. Instead, Kiara curled up and went to sleep.

Sharon took Kiara to the front of the class to demonstrate the first exercise, mainly to show my inadequacy as a dumb dog owner and also to prove that Kiara's problems were my fault and not hers. But Kiara refused to be coaxed, even when Sharon brought out the big guns of chopped liver. As Kiara already knew her name and the sit command, I called her back to me and told her to sit and she obediently did both. Sharon's mouth tightened and I fought hard not to cheer as I praised Kiara for being a good girl. It was the first time she'd responded to recall and I was ecstatic. Sharon then moved on to abuse some other poor woman's self-esteem. It was such an uneventful session that I was actually looking forward to doing the VAT return later.

Saturday 10 November
Ella's Movie-Making Birthday Party

I have ten nine-year-old girls for the afternoon, half of whom are scared of dogs, which means the pups have to spend the day shut in the living room behind the baby gate. Since dogs only ever want to be where the action is, this is going to be tantamount to torture for them. The volume level of ten young girls having fun is somewhere in the Hertz range of a thrash metal concert at Wembley Stadium. I split myself between filming the movie-making party (ironically) and making sure the pups didn't take their resentment out on any of the large furniture items we'd moved back into the living room. Apart from Kiara discovering that if she takes a long enough run up, she can leap straight over the baby gate, it all went pretty well. Kiara only appeared in two of the scenes which the director reassured us could be edited out later. I'll have to move the baby gate up higher tomorrow.

Sunday 11 November

Ivan is fuming. Kiara has destroyed four of his collectable records. The sleeves are untouched but the vinyl has more scratches than a Freddie Kruger victim. This time I know who it was because I caught them in the act of literally scratching, but not like a cool 80's hip-hop DJ.

Monday 12 November

Determined to find a day-care centre for the pups, I spent the morning phoning around every centre in the area. Most won't take Ridgebacks because they say "they don't enjoy the experience" which I'm pretty sure is code for "Ridgebacks are crazy, keep away!" I finally managed to get a viewing at Dave's Doggy Day-care and was invited to come along at lunch time, and bring the dogs along too. This sounded very hopeful! I checked the website and reviews and it all looked very impressive.

The grounds were set in woodland and were ideal for

the pups. The staff were friendly and knowledgeable and they smothered the pups with affection. One guy even managed to pick them up without putting his back out. The other dogs were clearly in their element playing in the woods. They asked if the pups would like to stay for the afternoon for a trial. I was torn between ecstasy at the thought of an afternoon to myself and mild anxiety at leaving them without warning. I agreed and said I'd pick them up after I collected Ella from school at 4.30 p.m.

The house was so quiet when I got home but also a complete mess so I used the time productively to give it a good clean. I'd forgotten the floor was a light oak! I washed their bedding and spent the rest of the day worrying if they were okay. I sent an email asking how they were doing and received a photo of them both alive and well.

It felt like a long afternoon for their first time at day care so I went a bit earlier to pick them up. I couldn't see anyone around so I let myself in through the main gate. Otis and Kiara were in a pen with a dozen or more other puppies. The minute they saw me they almost tore their limbs off to get to me. They raced down the track and catapulted themselves into the car. I was politely reprimanded for entering the premises and was told to ring the bell in future and wait for someone to bring the dogs out to me. When I asked why they were in the pen, I was told that puppies play in the pen until they're older and then move to the woods. So, they spent an afternoon in a concrete pen, half the size of our kitchen, with a dozen other crazy puppies. No wonder they looked stressed out of their minds.

Tuesday 13 November
Otis's First Puppy-Training Session

I was dreading having to see Sharon twice in one week, but to my delight, Tuesday's trainer was a warm bubbly lady called Nicky who genuinely liked dogs AND people. She introduced herself and we each introduced our dogs. Oddly, most owners had come as couples to this session and I felt like a single parent. There was a whole array of different breeds: Pugs, Dalmatians and, of course, Cockapoos. Not a single large dog. Otis looked completely out of place as he was at least double the size of the other puppies. As they darted into their owners' bags looking for treats, tried to escape or barked at the other puppies, Otis just sat there, calm and demure. He looked like he should be in senior school and not in kindergarten with this lot. The older couple next to me commented on how handsome Otis was and he turned to them as if to say, 'don't you know it'. Nicky asked if she could use Otis for a demonstration and I could not have been prouder as he performed his "sit" and "settle" perfectly. Admittedly, I had trained him in what I'd learnt from Kiara's session last Thursday, but I thought it best to omit that Kiara was his sister at this stage.

I was stunned at how well Otis, and even Kiara, behaved when they were away from each other. It was a hugely successful session and Otis picked up the commands so quickly that we moved on to "stay" and "leave it" before the class was finished. It made me realise how much simpler life would be with just one puppy. I could tell Otis really enjoyed the session and being away from Kiara was probably a relief for both of us.

As we left, Otis did an almighty wee which practically flooded the forecourt. As the owners filed out, they tried to steer their puppies around the river of steaming wee, gushing its way to the paddock. I pretended not to notice as the others attempted to jump over it to safety. What can I say – big dog, big bladder.

Wednesday 14 November

I'd agreed to give day care another try and was told that Wednesdays were quiet so they would have more space, and they'd also throw in some one-to-one training as an incentive. I couldn't refuse that. I'd told Ella I would make her school Mass at 11.00 a.m. so I dropped the pups off just before. When they saw the woods, they were beside themselves with excitement, anticipating a wondrous woodland walk. However, once I pulled up into the parking bay, all excitement dissipated. I rang the bell and was greeted by a charming young girl. I kissed the pups goodbye and left promptly. They pulled and pined to get back to me as she tried to jolly them along. I comforted myself in the fact that they were being socialised and that it was good for us to have a day apart, but I felt dreadful. Did they really hate it that much or did they just hate leaving me? I had no idea.

Mass was lovely and Ella beamed when she saw me. Singing hymns was just what I needed to take my mind off the pups. I did a big food shop and as I was collecting Ella's violin that afternoon (the place was near the day-care), it made sense to pick the pups up, too, albeit a bit earlier than I'd said. I followed protocol this time and tried not to look startled as the dogs pulled a young girl all the way down the dirt track as she hung on for dear life. She told me that Dave, the big boss, wanted to speak to me once I'd put the dogs in the car. Dave was about as far from a doggy day-care owner as I could imagine. Good looking, immaculate and the height of a munchkin. I noticed the row of sports cars with private number plates lined up behind him, all dog-related of course, and pondered how he could possibly make that much money looking after other people's mutts. Then I remembered the monthly payment plan I was roped into signing and the crammed puppy pen.

'I watched you this morning when you dropped your dogs off and saw you kiss them goodbye,' he said. 'They are not your children. They are your dogs, and need to be treated as such.'

Before I could interrupt, he went on, 'Kiara needs to go to boot camp. She has no boundaries and thinks she can do as she likes.' As if this was news to me. '*They* do not make the rules. You need to be tough with them,' he went on. 'These are not Cockapoos – they are huge guard dogs and need to be treated accordingly.'

'Okay,' I said. I felt like a twelve-year-old being bollocked by the headmaster and didn't know what else to say.

He glanced over at my car as two giant tongues licked the steamed-up window.

'And they shouldn't be in the back of the car. They should be in the boot where dogs belong.'

The boot? This isn't the 80s, I thought. We don't chuck kids and dogs in the boot of the car anymore. Then he softened and told me the name of a training camp to contact before cheerily waving goodbye.

I walked to the car muttering expletives under my breath as my eyes welled with tears. I hadn't strapped the pups in yet and they both pounced on me as I sat down, licking my face until all my tears and makeup were gone.

I Googled the company he mentioned and it looked like an SAS training camp. Surely Kiara wasn't that bad? She's still a puppy. She'll calm down.

Thursday 15 November

Kiara's second puppy-training session and I wasn't sure who hated it more – Kiara, me or Sharon. I had so much to do today I wondered if Sharon would warrant a busy day as a good enough excuse to skip today's lesson. I feared not. So, after a dental appointment, a quick run to the shops and doing the class Christmas hamper, I persuaded Kiara to get in the car for the forty-minute journey to training camp.

The moment Kiara realised where we were she curled herself into the size of a postage stamp and slid under the seat. I tried to entice her out of the car but even I sounded lacklustre. Awkwardly, we were the first in the training room and I had to make polite conversation with Sharon. I found out that she had nine rescue dogs (surprisingly) and that she lived alone (not surprisingly). All I could muster myself to say was, 'That must cost you a fortune! You must be working just to pay their food bill.' She didn't even answer me. Luckily the others arrived and we all sat in the same seats as last week. Titan was barking which I could see was already annoying Sharon as she began her droll instructions about this week's training session. Today we were going to learn, loose lead-walking and flat (which is lie down – something I felt like doing), but first we had a refresher of what we'd covered last week. However, it was clear that no one had done their homework and no one remembered a thing. This really pissed her off.

The session was generally mayhem, with none of the puppies doing what they were told and ended with Kiara making an escape attempt out of the open window. I wasn't expecting these sessions to be overwhelming fun, but I didn't think six puppies looking for an escape route was particularly encouraging. Only 4 more sessions to go. God help us.

Sunday 18 November

Took the pups for their first family walk in the woods. It was a gorgeous sunny day and the whole of Surrey's dog-walking population were out making the most of it. Ella was climbing on the huge branches and the pups ran after her wherever she went, excited at the space and new smells around them. The three of us ran off in different directions so the pups could run to each of us, giving them a good run to tire them out. We needn't have bothered, as we ended up getting completely lost and wandered around for hours trying to find our way back to the car park. The dogs were exhausted and we were starving. Then, seemingly out of nowhere, a horse came galloping towards us. Wide-eyed, we all looked at each other as we realised it was a fully grown Rhodesian Ridgeback. Having spotted his tribe, he tore towards us but Otis and Kiara, scared witless, ran as fast as they could in the opposite direction. When the owner caught up to their colossal beast and apologised to us (Otis and Kiara both hiding behind me, trembling), I asked how much he weighed. Fifty-five kilos, the woman told me. I was stuck for words. He was a dark chestnut with a large square head and looked very different to my two.

'What's his name?' I asked.

'Zeus,' she said. Perfect, I thought.

Eventually we found our car, got home and we all collapsed on the sofa. The pups slept until dinner time, they were so worn out. I Googled the average weight for Ridgebacks and thank the lord above that her dog was an exception. The average weight for females was 32 kilos and males, 38 kilos. Phew!

Tuesday 20 November

Otis's second training session, and he was so excited that he pulled me through the entire farm, overtaking all the other dogs, until we reached the training room. His sense of direction certainly needed no help but his queueing etiquette did. I'd read somewhere that it was best not to feed your puppy before training so they'll do anything for a treat, basically because they're starving. This was a mistake for two reasons:

1. Otis was so eager to take the treats from my hands that he took the skin off my fingers, and
2. the lure of tasty treats from five other puppy's goody bags was too much of a temptation for him.

I spent the majority of the session either wincing in pain or trying to distract him from darting off to nick other dog's treats every time we did a training lap. This was not a good time to do a recap of "leave it" when Otis's only intention was to fill his belly. To add insult to injury, hanging on the rack behind us was an array of tasty treats for sale which Otis was planning on looting. Needless to say, I will not be following this advice again, and I will also wear falconry gloves next week.

Thursday 22 November

It was Kiara's third training session and I was racking my brain for an excuse not to go. I was hoping for a bout of food poisoning or even a broken limb to get out of going, but as neither had occurred, we had to suck it up and take our punishment.

Kiara's dislike for people and dogs she doesn't know is

getting worse, and the place is full of both. She barks and darts around like a nutter from the moment we get out of the car.

This week, a new puppy has arrived called Gunther. And Gunther is a lunatic. He's like Kiara, only on speed. His owner is beside herself with anxiety and my heart goes out to her. He is so out of control that I actually don't know how this poor woman even made it out of the house sober. How she hasn't rehomed him is a miracle. Sharon certainly has her work cut out today and it's quite clear that no one is going to learn a thing. Instead, we'll be an audience learning how the hell you deal with a dog who's got a screw loose. Gunther was either lunging, barking, biting, jumping, spinning or hurling himself anywhere and everywhere. You had to see it to believe it. He made Kiara look normal. Sharon, cool as a cucumber put a muzzle on him. This made no difference. So, she ignored him and carried on with the class. This also made no difference. She made a fuss of him. Still no difference. Finally, she brought in a cage, put him in it and covered it with a giant fleece.

'I want everyone to ignore him until he calms down and only then will he be allowed to come out,' she shouted over his incessant barking.

Gunther spent the entire session in the cage. He was only let out at the end of the class, when he slipped his collar and made a run for it. We all left, leaving Sharon and his owner frantically trying to catch him. She was so pissed off I swear I could see steam coming out of her ears. I have a feeling Gunther won't be returning next week.

Tuesday 27 November

Otis is so smart that he's learnt the entire six-week foundation course by week three. This is partly due to the fact that as Kiara's sessions are ahead of his, I've been teaching him everything in advance.

Nicky is beaming at her star pupil and so today, as a special treat he is learning the trick of crawling through a long neon tube to conquer any fear of, well, crawling through a long neon tube. Otis completes it with utter aplomb. I was supposed to stand at the opposite end of the tube and entice him through with treats, but he'd gone straight through it and out the other side before I'd even got there. I'd like to say this was because he was so clever but actually it was because he was shit-scared and wanted to get it over with as soon as possible. I didn't blow his cover and let Nicky adorn him with his Star Pupil badge for the second week on the trot.

Thursday 29 November

As predicted, there is no Gunther this week. Either Sharon's banned him or his owner has checked into The Priory. This means that we are going to be the ones being shown up this time, as the other puppies are now starting to understand their training words and respond to them. Kiara is still hit and miss with pretty much everything Sharon has taught us. I've worked tirelessly at home teaching her the "stay" and "come" commands, but progress is slow to say the least. In class, Kiara is so unhappy she won't even take a treat, "high value" or not. I can see Sharon's patience level of virtually nil, going into negative figures with us now.

Today's lesson is on "impulse control" and I'm willing the session away before it's even begun. *My* impulse control is astonishingly high because I've wanted to tell Sharon where to stick it since week one. Kiara's, however, is dangerously low.

Sharon marches outside, commanding us to follow, and walks past the paddock to a field. A field full of horses. Although the horses are in the distance, Kiara is the first to spot them and turns from nervous puppy to serial killer in seconds as she crouches low in the assess-chase-kill stance. One of the horses walks towards us and, absurdly, Sharon tells us to come closer. I tell Sharon I don't think it's a good idea – even a novice can see that Kiara wants to kill the poor thing. But Sharon disagrees, and as I inch Kiara forward, she snaps and charges straight for the horse. As luck would have it, for the horse anyway, there is a chain-link fence between us and Kiara ploughs straight into it before hurtling backwards. I was furious as I knew this would happen. I was about to suggest ending the session when Sharon beat me to it.

'I think these sessions are too stressful for Kiara and not much benefit to her.' Which we all knew was code for, you're fired from puppy class. 'I'm sure the office will be happy to refund you for the final sessions and you might want to rethink it when she's a bit older.' And preferably in another country, she probably wanted to add.

How crazy was it that I had one puppy who was the star pupil of his class and another who was being kicked out? I felt sorry for Kiara as I looked at her, wide-eyed with stress.

'Come on, Kiara. Let's get you home.' She looked so relieved as we walked to the car.

I felt a pang of disappointment that she wouldn't be awarded her Puppy Foundation Certificate but this was eased by the fact that she would probably have eaten it on the way home anyway.

CHAPTER 5 – DECEMBER

JIMMY CHEWS

Age: 5 months
Weight: Otis 27.1 kg / Kiara 22.5 kg

Saturday 1 December

Cinderella goes to the Ball. Well, the school Ball, but quite honestly right now I'd settle for an Undertakers Ball. It's always a glitzy affair so it will be fun to get dressed up and make a change from my permanent attire of track-suits and welly boots. Ivan has surprised me by giving me my Christmas present early – a pair of beautiful satin burnt-orange Jimmy Choo shoes. I'd seen them earlier in the year and completely fallen in love with them but the price tag said, *you have two giant puppies to feed*, and so I'd put them out of my mind. But Ivan had snapped them up in a flash sale and now these beauties were mine. They will look gorgeous with my green velvet cocktail dress.

A long soak in the bath with two puppies lapping the bath water, followed by a slathering of body lotion being simultaneously licked off by two huge dog tongues wasn't quite the me-time I had in mind, but wherever I go, my two shadows are never far behind. Ella was excited to have Jane over to babysit although it's not my nine-year-old daughter who needs supervision. I make sure all the doors to the other rooms are closed and shut the pups in the living room with Jane and Ella, closing the newly raised baby gate behind me. Even at its new height it serves little purpose, as Kiara can spring right over it like Zebedee from the Magic Roundabout. Otis, being significantly heavier than Kiara, hasn't even attempted to jump over it and I think that even if he could, he probably wouldn't. He knows the purpose of the gate is to keep them in and is happy to follow the rules. Kiara's mission in life is to break them all.

I leave, knowing that the pups are in safe hands and feel confident that I can truly relax and enjoy the night. I clip-clop out the door in my stunning new heels ready to let my hair down and dance the night away.

Sunday 2 December

As far as I can remember, a good night was had by all. My head is thumping and I think I took letting my hair down to the extreme as I vaguely remember skidding over in front of Ella's headmistress.

It's 9 a.m. and I stagger to the kitchen to get the pups up. Ella has already let them out for a wee, bless her, and she's given them breakfast, but most surprisingly, both pups are sound asleep on the rug in the living room. Ella is in the kitchen making us toast which is just what I need to soak up this hangover. On my way to see the pups, I spot some unfamiliar shapes on the sofa. Without my contact lenses, I can't quite make them out and the hangover's not helping. I roll my eyes assuming yet another toy has met its fate in their clutches. But as I squint and move closer, the objects come into focus and my heart stops. I wasn't sure if the nausea was from the tequila shots or the dread of what I saw before me. As I stepped closer, I could see two orange straps and a chewed-up heel from my gorgeous new shoes which I'd kicked off when I got home and stupidly left on the living room floor! My brand-new beautiful shoes, worn for the very first and very last time. I felt sick and quickly smuggled them into my dressing gown so Ivan didn't see them. Ella jumped at the chance and asked if she could have them for dressing up. I can't believe my beautiful Christmas present has been relegated to the basket of nylon Disney wigs and plastic glitter wands after only one night in this world. Absolutely gutted.

Monday 3 December

A visit from the alarm company to do routine maintenance makes me wonder whether we actually need an alarm any more. The poor guy nearly had a heart attack after being "greeted" by Otis and Kiara who pinned him flat against the wall. It made me wonder what they might do should an intruder enter the house. The pups can sense a stranger before they've even entered the driveway, so any burglar would be out of their mind to try and break into this house. Mind you, there's not many valuables left to steal as the pair of them have destroyed most of them BAR.

Tuesday 4 December

I've lost count of the amount of toilet rolls Kiara has shredded. I wouldn't dream of putting one on an actual loo-roll holder any more, but it is annoying having to remember to get a loo roll out of the cupboard every time I need the toilet, and even more embarrassing when guests come over and have to call out for toilet paper.

The first few times Kiara ran around the house with a trail of loo roll behind her were cute and funny and we joked that she was like the Andrex puppy from the advert. But now we need shares in Andrex with the amount of rolls we're getting through. The dog eats four times a day so I've no idea why she needs to supplement her diet with mountains of bog roll.

Wednesday 5 December

No one prepares you for the hidden costs of having a dog. It's a bit like when you're having an extension built – there's the estimate and then there's the actual cost.

In the case of puppies, you budget for the initial cost, but what you are not prepared for are the additional expenses of training, specialists, day care, replacement of items destroyed, and all the other collateral damage. And if you're ever planning to leave the house *without* the dogs, then there is the hefty cost of the dog-sitter. I thought that one of the benefits of getting two dogs was that they would keep each other company. That they wouldn't get separation anxiety when you went out and that you could have a guilt-free day out or at the very least, a half-day out. This could not be further from the truth. What it actually means is that they are double trouble when they are together and so they need *more* supervision than if there was just one of them. And getting two puppies is not double the work – it's quadruple the work. And getting sibling puppies adds the further complication of the pack mentality which means they always have each other's backs. So, when one decides it's time to play up, the other one joins in. This makes looking after kids (and I've looked after dozens of challenging children when my parents fostered) an absolute doddle. With high-energy sibling puppies, you need the patience of a saint, the reflexes of a ninja, the stamina of an ox and eyes in the back, sides and front of your head.

Pros and Cons of having sibling puppies:

Cons

- Cannot train them together
- Cannot feed them together
- Cannot walk them together
- Any training done with one puppy will be undone by the other one
- Good habits will not be copied
- Bad habits will be copied and multiplied
- Household food bill will double
- Washing will triple
- House will be a pig-sty
- Bank account will be emptied
- Sanity will be lost

Pros

- They wash each other's ears

Friday 7 December

I love this time of year with all things Christmassy. I've been asked to help at Ella's school as Father Christmas is coming to visit the junior school and bringing live reindeer with him. I'm not sure why they think a woman with two crazy mutts is going to have more of a rapport with reindeer than the average Joe, but I'm looking forward to engaging with another species other than dogs.

My first impression is how small the reindeer are. Everything is relative and when you are living with two large brutes in the house, you no longer see things as you once did. Now when I see a cat, I am fascinated that a creature could be so small and delicate. When a friend's Schnauzer gives me his paw, it feels like a feather has floated into the palm of my hand. When Otis gives you his paw for a treat, it's like getting a low five from The Rock.

Saturday 8 December

We have a posh birthday bash tonight and won't be back until tomorrow. Ella is excited to be staying at a friend's house but I fear the pups won't be as excited to be spending the night at a dog hotel. I've no idea what a dog hotel actually is but the reviews are great and I've booked them the best VIP room. Check in is at 2.00 p.m. so I drive the dogs together in the back of the car for the forty-minute journey. I must admit I'm intrigued.

The journey is stressful as play fighting in the back of a car whilst being strapped into seatbelts is a dangerous activity for them, me and any passers-by. Kiara is jumping on Otis and slamming him into the window, and in traffic, fellow drivers look on aghast. I've given up telling them off and just blast Lenny Kravitz so I can't hear them.

Tonight will be their first night away from us and I'm pleased they have each other. The VIP room is a large room which they have all to themselves with their own private garden. It has underfloor heating, a sofa and music 24/7. I joked, asking if they had Sky TV and they said they're installing TVs next year! I've packed their favourite toys, their organic food and their bedding from home so they have a familiar smell. I've told the hotel not to provide any mattresses as Kiara eats them for breakfast. The lady who I spoke to was lovely and as they specialise in looking after rescue dogs, they shouldn't find these two too much trouble.

We arrive at the gate and are greeted by a guard dog who looks like Bigfoot. He is the biggest Husky-cross I've ever seen. Kiara and Otis aren't so cocky when they see him and sit down obediently in silence. I like this guard dog already. The pups are shown their room and look like they've been there a lifetime as they tear about the garden. Until I left. The howling, jumping and pounding at the door was agonising. But I told myself it's only one night and I'll be back first thing in the morning to collect them. I drove home with a huge knot in my stomach, feeling like I'd abandoned them. Then remembered I could get ready without worrying what they were up to, could have a bath by myself and could sit on the sofa with a glass of wine without being jumped on. And I could go to the loo on my own and actually put the loo roll on the holder! Bliss. I might have imagined it, but there was more wildlife in the garden too. It seemed that with the pups away and the mass extinction of British wildlife now off the menu, all the little creatures came back to enjoy the garden like something out of Snow White. We spent the afternoon playing Frozen Monopoly without interruption or calamities, just like the old days, pre-dogs. I asked Ella if she missed not having the pups around as it was so quiet and she said, 'No. I don't get to spend much time with you any more as you're always so busy with the dogs.' She looked so sad when she said this and I felt awful. Juggling a family, work and two overgrown puppies was taking its toll on all of us.

I decided to book a weekend away for the two of us in Brighton. A dog-free mini break for us girls to look forward to. We just needed to butter up Ivan to look after the dogs, so we let him win all the games before we broke the news to him.

Sunday 9 December

Waking up on a Sunday morning without Ella or the puppies is desolately quiet. I called Ella to say good morning but couldn't call the dogs for obvious reasons. Rather than making the most of the freedom I had, I set off to collect the puppies and Ella, leaving Ivan asleep in the luxury of no one to disturb him.

To say the pups were pleased to see me is an understatement. They went berserk. I have no idea what possessed me to wear white jeans but they were heading straight for the bin when I got home. There was no stain remover strong enough to even bother attempting it, but I didn't care. I was as pleased to see them as they were to see me. I gathered up their things and asked for their toys to take back with us as these were the only things missing.

'I'm afraid there's not much left of them and we thought it best to remove them to avoid choking hazards,' the girl said. 'But they're in the office if you'd like to take them.'

A pile of decimated remains was handed to me in a poo bag. I'd spent a fortune on those so-called 'indestructible' toys. They'd only had them for one night! A fleeting thought about taking them back to the shop crossed my mind but carrying a poo bag of unidentifiable rubber, fluff and rope into the shop didn't seem appropriate as I spend half my life there these days, so I just wrote off yet another batch of toys. I'm really going to have to find some more durable toys for them to chew.

Monday 10 December

Ella and I went to our local charity shop on the way home from school to see what we could buy which the pups might like to destroy and would only cost a few quid. Ella had a lightbulb moment when she suggested getting them some shoes, as they seem hell-bent on chewing any shoe we leave in sight. I try to contain my excitement at both the range and price of shoes on sale. The strappy gold evening sandals are perhaps not the most suitable chew toys although I'm pretty sure a dog trainer would say any shoe is unsuitable since it will only exacerbate their shoe fetish. But then I spot a pair of red patent-leather loafers which are just perfect. My size too! I felt guilty buying a pair of Italian loafers for £3 just for the dogs to chew.

'You're not going to tell the lady what they're for, are you?' Ella asked me, slightly panicking.

'Of course not. I'm going to tell her they're for me.' And I slipped them on. Ella cringed.

'I'm going to wear them when I pick you up from school later,' I joked.

They were such a hit with the pups – they couldn't get enough of them! And the beauty was that with a pair of shoes, they had one *each*! You couldn't buy a dog chew for that price.

On the success of this, Ivan returned to the shop and came back with an entire cardboard box full of old ladies' shoes which we are going to ration out throughout the week. I have added a note to the box so that, if I die before these shoes are all eaten, whoever is clearing out the house knows that these were NOT MY SHOES! I may die looking like I've been dragged through a hedge backwards, but I would like to leave this world with at least a shred of my fashion taste intact.

Wednesday 12 December

I love cold, blindingly bright winter mornings like these. I relish the first few moments of complete calm before the chaos ensues. Ivan and Ella were still asleep. I didn't want to wake them but I knew the moment the pups sensed I was up they would start yowling. As it wasn't 6.00 a.m. yet we could play in the garden as no other dogs would be up.

I opened the patio doors first then opened the pups' crates and they shot out like missiles. Once Otis released his usual tank of wee, he chased after Kiara who ran so fast, he could barely keep up. The speed at which these two run is astonishing. When they are fully grown, they can run as fast as a greyhound at 30 km per hour, and they don't look far off that speed already. What amazes me is that they can stop dead in a split second. They are so dextrous with their turns and dodges that they never bump into anything or anyone, fortunately for us. It's like watching parkour for dogs, the way they chase and dodge each other at play. Kiara uses sheer strength and speed and Otis uses strategy and tactics. He can predict where Kiara is going to emerge and takes short cuts to catch her out, so although she's faster, his stamina is superior, and when she's panting and looking for water, he can keep going. In fact, I've never seen Otis out of breath. It's clear that he's the brains and she's the brawn, and if these two were in their ancestral plains of Africa, they wouldn't need a pack to help them chase and contain a lion. They could do it alone. The perfect pairing. The yin and the yang in complete harmony working together.

Thursday 13 December

I'm off to a funeral today. I glance at the calendar and realise it would have been Kiara's final puppy-training class. Thank heavens for small mercies. Even a funeral is more enjoyable than that class. My friend Gemma is dog-sitting and the pups will be over the moon to see her. They are so attuned to what's going on around them, despite their craziness, that I can't even mention Gemma's name without them reacting. They already have a list of words they recognise as long as my arm. People's names are a new skill they've learnt recently. And it's nothing to do with the tone I use. I could be having a conversation and just make a comment about Gemma, and both heads pop up at the mere mention of her name. Otis runs to the front door, thinking that she's about to arrive and waits until I distract him. The same with my cousin Amber. They run to the kitchen door if they hear us say her name as they know this is the door she comes in. Otis once spent fifteen minutes waiting at the door for Amber because I'd mentioned she was cutting my hair later. He looked out of the window when every car went past, hoping it was her, and didn't settle until she arrived three hours later. Now that they're so sensitive to conversation, we have to remember to either silently mouth their names or spell them out to prevent them getting excited. Although it probably won't be long before they can spell.

Today I can let them know that Gemma is coming and they bolt to the front door, greeting her with their usual fanfare of jumping up and licking her all over. Rule #6 "No Jumping Up" still needs work, but Gemma looks as happy to be with them as they are with her.

I change into my black skirt, roller off a layer of auburn dog hairs and back out of the door before they add any more. I watch as they hang onto Gemma's every word and fight for her attention, scrambling around, finding as many toys as they can to show off to her. They don't even notice I've gone. I can truly relax when the pups are in good hands especially with someone who really loves them.

Friday 14 December

It's Mum's birthday and we're going out for a curry tonight. It's also the last day of term and Ella is finishing at midday. We usually go out for the afternoon but as the pups can't be trusted for both the afternoon and the evening, Ella is having a friend over after school instead.

I promised Ella that I'd bring the pups to school at pick up as her teacher wanted to meet them. It's a novelty for kids to show off their puppies at school but these tend to be small dogs which can be smuggled into the playground in a handbag. These pups would struggle to fit into a suitcase. I did consider bringing them in a wheelbarrow but noticed a new sign on the school gate, "No dogs allowed on school grounds". They must have heard we were coming. I wouldn't dream of taking these two into a playground filled with excitable kids running around. Otis and Kiara would think they were in heaven as they chased and terrorised every child and teacher out of the playground. The plan was for her teacher to come and meet them in the car. The pups were as confused as they were excited, as the car became surrounded by kids and their parents. Ella's teacher pushed through the crowd and nearly swore when she saw the size of them.

'How old did you say they were?' she asked, shocked.

'Five months,' I said.

'I think you're going to need a bigger car!'

Ella squeezed into the back with the pups for the drive home so her friend could sit in the front seat. I couldn't even see Ella in my rear-view mirror as both Kiara and Otis were on top of her, excited to see her after three hours of being away. Having a couple of playmates for the pups might enable me to get a bit of work done before we go out tonight.

'Muuuuummmmmyyyyyy!' I heard Ella shout from the kitchen. I rushed in and Otis came running up to me with his playful growl, offering me his latest gift – a large carving knife which had been left in the sink last night. I guess they must have grown a few more inches as they can now reach into the kitchen sink. Yet another zone to be puppy-proofed. Maybe leaving a couple of nine-year-olds in charge of them wasn't such a great idea.

Saturday 15 December

After debating whether to put up a Christmas Tree this year with two mad dogs living in the house, we decided that it just wasn't Christmas without one. Even though the rest of the house was decorated and looked beautiful, there was a gaping space where the tree should be. Ella and I went to Squires and found a large, plush Norway Spruce which would make the house complete, and more importantly, didn't drop its needles. Decorating the tree together is a yearly ritual we love. We put on Michael Bublé's Christmas album, I pour myself a glass of fizz and we dance around, decorating the tree together with our collection of beautiful baubles we've collected since Ella was tiny. As Ivan had a lie-in this morning, he was happy to look after the pups while we returned to Squires to pick out some special Christmas baubles to commemorate this year with our new family members.

Ella chose a delicate fairy queen and a smaller glass fairy which reminded her of the two of us. I bought a couple of beautiful glass dog baubles to commemorate our first Christmas with the pups. As there were no Ridgeback baubles (presumably the tree would topple over under the weight), a couple of Pugs had to do. The plan was to put them high up out of harms reach. We picked up some dog treats while we were there and I left the bag with everything in it on the kitchen counter.

Sadly, the fairies nor the Pugs made it to the tree. They were found smashed to pieces on the floor, along with an empty packet of dog treats. They will instead be replaced with two cat baubles made of titanium.

Sunday 16 December

We are still unpacking the leftover boxes from the kitchen extension. I cannot believe how much stuff we have accumulated in our five years here. There are more vases, cook books and packets of pasta than we have space to put them, even with the new extension. But it is probably time to figure this out as every time I walk into the kitchen, the pups have found another way of opening a box – usually by ripping off one side – and distributing the contents over the floor, then either rolling in it, eating it or more often, both. Today it looks like they have a dreadful case of dandruff as they are both covered in white flakes which the leftover chewed-up packet on the floor confirms is panko breadcrumbs from one of the boxes.

Monday 17 December

Kiara had a busy night unstuffing her mattress again so all that was left was a sorry-looking empty woollen sack and a crate full of polyester stuffing. She had pulled the fleece, which was covering her crate, through the bars and into her bed, and proceeded to chew on this whilst screwing her bed blanket into a ball in the corner. Otis's mattress was untouched. His bed was so perfect it looked like he'd made it when he got up.

I took Otis to a Tricks Training class tonight which Nicky was running. He learnt "stay" from a distance (useful), slalom (potentially useful) and skateboarding (not useful but SO cool). I admit that when I saw the skateboard I did wonder how on earth he was going to do this and also, what was the actual point. I can't see what sort of situation we would ever be in when a skateboarding dog would prove to be useful, but apparently, as well as learning confidence, it teaches them balance. Nicky thought being such a large dog he would struggle and that his weight would tip the board, but he was bloody awesome and he loved it. Admittedly, I wasn't about to take him to a skate park any time soon, but he could put three legs on it and push himself along with the other for a few metres. I wanted to take a video of him but no phones were allowed. So, instead, I sent Ivan a video of a similar-looking dog skateboarding like a pro and he thought it was Otis! Nothing like high expectations. I was thinking of buying Otis a skateboard for Christmas but I fear Kiara would eat it.

Wednesday 19 December

Christmas is around the corner and I still have so much to do. I rush the pups to their monthly weigh-in at the vets which is the opposite of Weight Watchers as the aim here is to gain weight. Otis is now 27.1 kilos and Kiara 22.5, so no worries there. I could just about pick them up, but more as a challenge than as an affectionate gesture. I collected the myriad of pills and potions for worming, fleas, ticks and lungworm and avoided any head-on incidents with pets in the waiting room.

I took the pups to the park for a quick run before starting on my list of 100 things still to do before Christmas. In the park, Kiara chased literally everything. Just lately she's developed the compulsion to chase anything and everything, be it human, animal or object, and it is impossible to stop her. On the one hand, it does tire her out which means she's less manic for the rest of the morning, but on the other, she is terrifying people and their pets and, at worst, is going to get herself and possibly others killed in the process. I'm going to have to put her on lead in the park until I can get this behaviour under control.

Thursday 20 December

I've got a stinking cold and now it feels like it's going to my chest. Perfect timing with Christmas just five days away. But when you have kids or pets, you just have to get on with it, dose yourself up with Paracetamol and hope that will do the trick, and if it doesn't, it's tough luck as you still have to get on with it anyway.

We are supposed to be going to see the Christmas lights in London tonight with friends but I'm not up to it, so Ivan's taking Ella without me. This gives me some time to wrap the gifts from Santa with my attentively unhelpful little elves, Otis and Kiara.

Sunday 23 December

I'm starting to feel better, although I have a hacking cough which makes me sound like a sixty-a-day smoker. It does stop the pups in their tracks when they're doing something naughty though, so I'm using it to my advantage.

Doing the Christmas food shop is not usually something I relish but even the mayhem of being amongst 20 million stressed-out shoppers in Sainsbury's is more relaxing than trying to get any chores done with the pups around.

If I have absolutely nothing to do (i.e. when I'm dead) and give the pups my undivided attention, then they are as good as gold, but as I have a life – a busy one at that – they use any opportunity to tear the place apart. If they are not napping in their crates, then they are a couple of lunatics. Kiara tears around the place, barking at thin air, grabbing whatever she passes – like a scarf or a cherished nursery painting on the wall – and devours it in a nanosecond. The only safe place to leave them without supervision would be a padded cell. I didn't have to baby-proof a single thing when I had Ella, but I have to puppy-proof practically everything with these two.

After unpacking the Christmas shopping under the close scrutiny of Otis and Kiara, I set the table so that it's not a mad rush tomorrow. I gave the pups their decoy – two hefty chew bars which they fought over for fifteen minutes even though they were identical – and started making the nut roast and pastry for dessert. Kiara lost interest in her chew and found stealing whatever I put on the table and running off with it way more fun. After every napkin had been nicked, I gave her one of her own but Otis grabbed it, ran into the garden and weed on it, so now she wants another. I found some paper ones for Kiara which she enjoyed immensely and made damn sure her brother couldn't get hold of any of these. Then she started taking the cutlery off the table. Each time I sternly told her, NO, she would stop, look at me, quickly grab it and run off. At least Otis waits until my back is turned. In the end, I shut them both out of the living room and let them have the run of the kitchen and garden by themselves. Generally, in life, the busier your day, the more life throws at you. Somewhere in the garden the dogs found fox poo and took it in turns to roll in it and smear it around the kitchen. I am standing in the kitchen in my knickers and bra, having bathed them both twice, when Ivan comes in,

‘I hope that’s not the nut roast I can smell.’

‘No, it’s the smell of “next year we are going out for Christmas lunch!”.’

Monday 24 December – Christmas Eve

A lovely evening at the church service, with Ella and her friends joining in the Nativity and us happily singing Christmas carols. The pups are in their crates and I don’t have to worry, so all is well in the world. As tempting as it is to accept the offer of going to the pub afterwards, I still have to wrap presents and give the pups their last meal. I read Ella a story and repeatedly tell the pups they can’t jump on the bed and join us – it’s not circle time. Ella falls straight to sleep. She must be the only child on the planet who sleeps on Christmas Eve, and us the only parents who get a lie in on Christmas Day! I pour myself a generous Merlot and put on a bit of Mr Bublé. I finish wrapping, with the pups fighting over any paper or ribbon that falls, while I happily sing along to Michael’s Christmas album. I won’t even let the remains of one of my wedding shoes in Kiara’s bed (no idea how she got hold of that) ruin the evening.

The tree is still in one piece, the presents wrapped and the food all prepared. The house looks lovely – I did it! And actually, I am really looking forward to tomorrow. My parents, brother, Jane and her mum are joining us, and it’s our first Christmas with the pups. Ella is beyond excited and she’s bought the pups lots of presents which she’s sensibly hidden under her bed in a locked box so that they don’t open them before the big day.

Tuesday 25 December – Christmas Day

Christmas lunch is all about the timing, so I'm up at the crack of dawn to make sure everything stays on schedule. My dad, having never even boiled an egg, will expect dinner the minute he steps through the front door.

I'd bought the pups sparkly velvet collars for the day. Kiara's is purple and Otis's is black, and they looked so cute wearing them for all of ten minutes. Kiara yanked Otis's collar over his head then ran around with it before flinging it into the garden. Then she slipped her own one over her head and chewed it before I confiscated it. They definitely weren't dogs who were into dressing up. Instagram-worthy photos were a far cry, not that I had any time for social media on top of everything else.

Ella gave the pups their presents which were stockings full of toys and treats. I took out the toys, knowing they would be decimated before I'd finished peeling the potatoes, and let them have the treats instead. I left them in the packets so they could spend some time ripping them open while we opened our presents. But their teeth are so sharp they tore the packets open in one slick move. Otis wanted Kiara's treats and Kiara wanted his, so I swapped them over and they changed their minds again. I flung both packets over my shoulder and let them fight it out between them. This kept them busy for a while at least.

The nut roast I'd made last night was still intact (an advantage of being vegan) so I hurriedly got dressed and continued getting lunch ready before everyone arrived, leaving the pups and Ella playing with all the new and exciting toys. The pups had bought Ella a Make Your Own Pottery Kit which was very thoughtful, considering Kiara had eaten her last one.

When everyone was here, I made sure that every door

to every single room was closed as it was impossible to keep an eye on the pups whilst sorting out lunch. Ivan was getting everyone drinks so we couldn't close the baby gate as we needed to keep going back and forth between the kitchen and living room. This meant the pups had access to the kitchen, living room and hallway only. With all the fuss, they fell fast asleep on their rugs during lunch. Otis was behind Jane's chair in the living room and Kiara on her rug in the hallway, where I could keep a safe eye on her.

And then she was gone.

'Where's Kiara?' I did a rapid scan of the living room.

'She's on her rug in the hall,' Ivan answered without looking up.

'No, she's not.' I tried to keep the panic out of my voice.

I bolted out of my seat and was relieved to see all the doors to the bedrooms and bathroom were still closed. I called her name, nothing. I checked the kitchen and garden but she wasn't there either. I opened each bedroom door one by one but she was nowhere to be seen. My bedroom was the last room to check. Unless she'd magically transported herself to another place, there was nowhere else she could be. I slowly opened the door and there before me was the carnage I feared. Kiara was lying on the floor, surrounded by open shoe boxes and a pile of chewed-up designer shoes. She had taken one shoe out of each box and chewed it up, leaving the other one of each pair in their box, perfectly intact. All four pairs of my beautiful Jimmy Choos – which I'd collected over years – destroyed in ten minutes flat. All I could wonder was what was wrong with the other shoe in each box? Couldn't she have eaten the pair? Then at least I'd have one or two pairs left. But nothing about this dog made sense.

'Kiara!' I said slowly, 'what have you done?' She looked up at me, picked up a four-inch decapitated heel, and handed it to me with a playful growl. I know I should have gone nuts and probably banned her from joining us, but it wouldn't make any difference. She wouldn't understand. She would just hide behind the sofa then do it again. I let her out of my bedroom and she trotted down the hallway to join the others.

'Have you found her?' came the echo from around the table.

'Yes,' I said.

'What has she done?' Ivan asked.

'You don't want to know,' I said, and sat down to eat my lunch.

I loved those shoes, and if someone had told me a year ago they would be chewed up by a puppy with a Choo fetish, I would have cried a river. But it was fair to say my attachment to material things was becoming less important now that they were all rapidly disappearing.

I did a quick scout around the floor and locked everyone else's shoes in Ella's bedroom for safe keeping. I'm not sure others would have my tolerance level regarding Kiara's shoe obsession.

Wednesday 26 December – Boxing Day

My brother offered to pup-sit today so we could go and see the Mary Poppins musical.

What I'd pay for a magical umbrella that could whisk me up, up and away.

Friday 28 December – Girls Weekend in Brighton

Ella and I were so excited to spend a fun weekend together in Brighton. It's one of our favourite places to go. We booked into The Grand Hotel as a special treat and got upgraded to a huge suite with a double balcony overlooking the sea. It was gorgeous. The sun shone all weekend and we relished every moment. We wandered the Lanes buying crystals and dried flowers, went on the rides on the pier and ate candyfloss. Ella convinced me to go in the Upside-down House and get vertigo but I drew a line at the zip wire! We rode the carousel and on the beach we bumped into a young girl walking a Ridgeback. It's like being in a club when you have a Ridgie, and we couldn't resist running over to say hello. Her name was Tulla and she was so gentle and calm. She was twenty months old and was as good as gold. I sighed when I thought of our two. Ella enthusiastically told her about Otis and Kiara and they sounded like complete nutters, but it was so sweet the way she spoke about them. Ella absolutely loved the pups but I could tell being here with her mama meant so much to her. It was something we both really needed and I vowed to do more of.

Monday 31 December – New Year's Eve

In case the pups got freaked out by the fireworks, we wanted to stay in with them tonight. Ella was having a sleepover at her friend's house so it was just me, Ivan and the pups. I'd heard all sorts of stories about how stressed dogs get with fireworks so I'd armed myself with all the necessary tools to keep them relaxed, which included:

- a Kalms spray
- a plug-in de-stresser with pheromones
- classic FM playlist
- earplugs (for me) should the barking become deafening

The first blast from our neighbour's house was so loud,

I jumped out of my skin. Both pups came up to me to check that I was okay. Missile after missile went off and were so loud it sounded as though they were right outside the window. I swear fireworks get louder every year. The pups weren't scared in the slightest, but looked confused as to where the sounds were coming from and tried peeking behind the curtains. I opened the living-room curtains fully so they could see them and they both watched, transfixed, as one colourful explosion went off after another. Kiara followed each stream of light as it fell from the sky and disappeared behind the trees. She looked at me as if to say, where have they gone?

By 11 p.m., Ivan was tired and went to bed so it was just me and the pups seeing in the New Year together. As they were having so much fun, I cracked open a bottle of bubbly and the three of us sat cuddled up on the sofa watching the incredible fireworks display as the clock struck midnight. My phone beeped with New Year messages and I held up my glass to the pups and said, 'Here's to a New Year with less stress, less mess and more progress!'

CHAPTER 6 – JANUARY

PARK BAN!

Age: 6 months
Weight: Otis 30 kg / Kiara 27 kg

Tuesday 1 January

New Year's Resolutions

1. We will not jump up and knock people over when they walk through the front door
2. We will not stand on the table before, during or after our family's dinner
3. We will not eat family or friends' shoes, however tasty they may look
4. We will not eat Ella's toys: small, large, glow-in-the-dark or otherwise
5. We will not destroy household items such as sofas, utensils or remote controls (apparently extremely important judging by parent's reaction)
6. We will not eat office items, including cables, pens and Post-its
7. We will not eat gardening items like gloves, pots and compost
8. We will not devour loo rolls, mattresses, cushions or any other form of stuffing
9. We will not eat each other's food as it is exactly the same

Wednesday 2 January

We are off to London to see Ella's friend in A Christmas Carol. My folks are coming to pup-sit for the day. I told the pups, 'Nana and Grandpa are coming,' and the second they heard their car on the gravel drive they catapulted to the door and launched themselves at them. After jumping up and breaking their first New Year's Resolution, I attempted to run through the list of instructions I'd made to help my parents communicate with the pups and avoid any incidents.

Words to be said in light-hearted and enthusiastic manner:

come here
outside
wee wees
in your bed
biscuit
dinner
sit
good boy/ girl

Words to be said firmly:

off
drop (works 50 % of the time)
leave it (works 0% of the time with Kiara)

With both parents enjoying being licked and mauled, and neither one of them listening to a word I was saying, I checked all the bedroom and bathroom doors were locked and headed out. Ivan was already in the car with the engine running.

'Call me with any problems,' I said, 'and if you can't see them, then they're up to no good. Silence means trouble.'

After a fabulous show, we returned home to no incidents.

'They've been no trouble at all,' my mum said proudly. 'Nothing destroyed.' She beamed. You'd hope if your only job is to watch two puppies for four hours – with a bit of TV thrown in and the odd glass of wine – that the house would remain in one piece, and luckily it did.

'That's great,' I said and I meant it. I was sincerely hoping I'd found a new dog-sitting duo.

When I went into the bathroom, an entire twelve-pack of toilet rolls had been demolished, along with a body lotion, sponge and decapitated Barbie doll, breaking three out of the nine New Year's resolutions in one go! I didn't have the heart to tell them. Sometimes ignorance is bliss, especially if you're looking for a new dog-sitter.

Friday 4 January

Amber came over to cut our hair. She loves the pups and they love her hairdressing paraphernalia like scissors, bleach and clipper cord. We have to take it in turns to puppy sit whilst the other is getting their hair cut to avoid a visit to the emergency vets. It's not quite the relaxing experience it once was (pretty much like everything these days).

At least in terms of grooming the pups couldn't be anymore low maintenance. My friends pay a small fortune taking their dogs to the groomers to get a wash, cut and blow dry. Otis and Kiara's coats are self-cleaning. The mud on their bodies just dries and falls off, and as they clean each other's ears, there's not much left for me to do in terms of grooming apart from cleaning their eyes and clipping their nails – which is always a drama. I have taught the pups the word "eyes" and when I say this, they squint and tilt their heads so that I can wipe the sleep from them. It's very cute. Once I teach them to wipe their feet when they come in and not smear mud over every inch of the house, it will be job done!

How to clean eight muddy paws before entering the house:

1. place four large bath towels inside patio door
2. let one dog in without decapitating the other one
3. hold said dog still whilst trying to wipe paws, while other dog throws themselves at patio door
4. accidentally knee dog in the chest whilst trying to stop him jumping in your face
5. grab dog by the collar as attempts to escape, wiping mud all over dressing gown and slippers
6. shout at other dog to stop barking and scratching new glass door
7. wipe mud off self, whilst being licked and head-butted by dog
8. let other dog in and repeat
9. break up play fighting whilst continuing to wipe mud off self
10. sprint to shut living-room door before they get there and spread mud all over all furniture
11. throw muddy slippers away, along with previous life.

Sunday 6 January

Kiara has perfected a brand-new skill this year, especially to wind Ivan up – digging holes in his beautiful lawn. Actually, they are nearer in size to craters than holes. I discovered this last night when I went out into the garden to make sure they'd done a wee before bed, and disappeared down one. With Kiara's talons growing faster than Jack's beanstalk, the speed at which she can dig is astonishing. I let her out first thing this morning and caught her in the act. It looked like something out of a cartoon, her front paws burrowing away at speed and dirt flying through the air and landing in mounds around her. When I rushed outside and told her 'NO!', she dove head first into the dirt and rolled around in it, kicking her legs in the air. Otis could see how much fun she was having and started digging his own hole. 'Otis, NO. STOP IT!' I shouted, and he did. He looked gutted that he was being denied this fun game but while I was outside, he didn't try it again. Kiara, on the other hand, went straight over to a new patch of freshly mown, pristine lawn and did it again, right in front of me. I sternly told her, 'NO', and she ignored me again, so I took her inside.

Ivan went mad. 'I thought you said Ridgebacks don't dig!' which I presumed was more of a statement than a question.

'That's what the books said,' I offered, weakly. Pretty much everything the books said about Ridgebacks was factually incorrect when it came to Kiara. I tried to assure Ivan that all puppies dig and that she will grow out of it. He filled in the holes, silently seething, and I had to admit, the lawn looked awful. He stood there looking out at the garden and I could feel his pain. 'This garden used to look stunning,' he said sadly, without adding, before these effing dogs.

The once vibrant green lawn, voluminous tropical plants and blossoming flower beds had turned into a muddy, ripped-up lawn covered in holes, yellow wee stains, trampled-on tropical plants, half-eaten flowers and chewed-up dog toys. If a bunch of Travellers had turned up and set up camp, I wouldn't have been surprised.

Kiara wound herself around Ivan's legs.

'Look what you've done, Kiara,' he said, exasperated, and stroked her.

'She's not doing it to be naughty,' I said. But I couldn't be sure. It was a miracle he was being as understanding as he was, given that he loved his lawn as much as he loved us. I will find a way to make it up to him and I will find a way to make this bloody dog listen to me if it's the last thing I do.

Monday 7 January

The physical work involved with bringing up two large dogs is more than I imagined, and it's certainly taking its toll on my body. The constant cleaning, washing of the floor, bedding and fleeces, the strain from them pulling on the lead, the energy I need to walk them multiple times a day, in addition to the stress of their behaviour, is absolutely knackering me out. I thought a beneficial new year's resolution for *me* would be to start each day with some daily yoga to calm the mind, loosen the joints and strengthen the body.

How to do yoga with two Rhodesian Ridgeback puppies:

Step 1 – locate pieces of yoga mat which have not been entirely shredded by sharp puppy teeth
Step 2 – attempt to lay said pieces on the floor without pups playing tug of war with them
Step 3 – lie on the mat whilst being walked over, licked and scratched
Step 4 – lock dogs out of living room so that you can get on with yoga
Step 5 – let dogs back in to stop yowling, whining and clawing at the door

Step 6 – attempt to distract dogs by throwing toys and lie back on mat
Step 7 – fight dogs off whilst they try to take mat out from under you
Step 8 – abort all attempts at yoga, switch on TV and watch Lorraine with a cup of tea or preferably something stronger

Wednesday 9 January

Kiara has eaten my glasses. It would have been handy to have a spare pair before she did this, as they do prove quite useful for things like driving, watching TV and spotting her when she disappears on a walk (although this could be a great excuse to come home without her!). However, I hated those glasses and have been looking for a reason to buy a new pair for ages.

I've made an emergency appointment at the opticians to get a new pair, although these will take a couple of weeks which means wearing my contact lenses until then. The prescription for my lenses is a little out of date by about twenty years, so I'll have to keep an even closer eye on Kiara until my new specs arrive. I'm going to ask the optician if I can get some titanium frames with bionic lenses so that I can spot potential wildlife on the horizon before Kiara does.

Thursday 10 January

The garden is ready for winter. Ella has wrapped all my mini cannas and other tropical plants in their winter fleeces to protect them from the frost, and I have planted new tulip bulbs, which Jane bought me for my birthday. The pups have been showing a little too much interest in both of these activities so I am teaching them the command "leave it". Whenever they come close to the wrapped plants, I say, 'Leeeeave it,' and praise them when they back off. So far it seems to be working, although I did catch Kiara digging up a few bulbs when I wasn't looking (which I told Ivan was the squirrels). I have now covered the tulip pots with metal grates, making them both squirrel and Kiara-proof. As tempted as the pups were to unwrap the cannas from their cosy fleeces, they have unbelievably left them alone. Progress perhaps?

Friday 11 January

I still put the pups in their crates when I go out, both for their own safety and to limit any vandalism. Leaving them loose, even for a short while, always ends in disaster. But today, they've both had a really long walk and I feel mean disturbing them from their deep sleep. They don't even stir when I pick up my keys so I risk leaving them loose while collecting Ella from school.

It was not a risk worth taking. I came home to two wide-awake puppies looking up at me over the gate, gleefully proud of what they'd done. Amongst the usual ripped-up toilet tissue which they'd shredded into a million pieces, there was toilet cleaner all over the rug, with dog vomit mixed in. They'd evidently decided to drink some, and lucky for them, it was a toxic-free toilet cleaner or things could have been a lot worse. Kiara must have jumped over the gate which is now at its maximum height of nearly 4 feet (!!!), grabbed bathroom supplies and jumped back over so she could drag Otis into her mess. Getting vomit and loo cleaner out of a thick-pile rug is a pretty challenging task as the whole lot turns to a foaming volcano of vomit and slime. It took me two hours to get the disgusting mess out and the room reeked for the rest of the evening. Ella and Ivan ate their dinner in the kitchen and I spent the evening in the living room with the pups, inhaling the stench of dog vomit and lemongrass.

Saturday 12 January

Ella has refused to come with me to walk the pups, saying that it scares her. And Ivan isn't keen either. I can't really blame them as the last few times have been a total nightmare.

Since the "family walk" is just me today, I left early before the other dog-walkers were out. I wanted to give Kiara one last chance at being off lead so I went to the quiet hotel with the large grounds. It was completely deserted. I unclicked the lead and Kiara trotted along beside me with Otis. But somewhere over the hill and far away, not visible to the human eye, Kiara had spotted a man with a dog, and before I could stop her, she was gone. In a flash, she was over the hill and out of sight, along with her back-up buddy, Otis. All I could hear was their incessant barking in the distance. I ran as fast as I could up the hill until I could barely breathe. Far ahead of me was a furious red-faced man and his terrified dog being circled and barked at by two crazed Ridgebacks.

'Get your FUCKING dogs under control!' he screamed from across the grounds.

I shouted for them in every voice possible as I continued running towards them.

Otis came galloping back but Kiara ignored me and continued jumping around, barking at the man. He kicked her and instead of running back to me like a normal dog, she jumped up, pulled his backpack off and ran off with it. The man ran after her, screaming his lungs out, with

Otis now chasing after him. With everyone's adrenaline pumping, I didn't know what to do. It was out of control. Kiara lost her grip on the backpack and hurtled towards me, followed by Otis and all three of us ran as fast as we could back to the car, with the man in hot pursuit. It was the fastest I've run since school sports day.

I was shaking and sweat was pouring down my back. The man was enraged and catching up with us. I fumbled to open the car and Otis and Kiara bolted into the back, and we shot out of there like a scene from *The Fast & The Furious*. When we reached the main road, I burst into tears – big loud sobs – and couldn't stop. Otis watched me and tried to lick my face. Kiara, her adrenalin still pumping, had her face squashed up to the window and was barking at people as we drove past.

'KIARA, NO!' I shouted.

'KIARA, STOP IT!'

But she didn't stop. She barked at every dog, every person, every bird and every squirrel the whole way home as tears just streamed down my face. I didn't understand this dog. Nothing I did was working. She was a law unto herself. She was making life impossible and I had no idea what to do.

Sunday 13 January

I am treating today as God intended it – as a day of rest. I am emotionally and physically wrecked and I am not taking the dogs out today. It's clear they can't be walked together any longer. Kiara is uncontrollable and the pack instinct is too strong (okay, so some of the books were right).

Ivan and Ella have taken over dog duties, including their four feeds, so that I can have the day off. The pups want nothing more than to be with me and scratch at my bedroom door all morning. I know they are not purposefully making my life a misery but I need to figure out a way to deal with this situation. Today, however, I don't have the strength for it. I can relax knowing that, at least in the safety of our home, where humans outnumber animals, it will be an event-free day.

Monday 14 January

The high-energy nature of Ridgeback puppies means that if we skip a walk, I pay for it later. Ideally, they need to be walked twice a day, once for exercise and once for mental stimulation AKA sniffari – a walk with plenty of smells. As I can no longer walk them together for fear of death or police arrest, it means I am going to have to do four separate thirty-minute walks a day. Running a house, working, keeping on top of Ella's extracurricular activities and preventing the house from looking like a dosshouse whilst doing four walks, is going to be a challenge. And unless I'm planning on doing the washing at midnight, I am going to require some help.

A busy holiday period means I've pretty much pulled in all the dog-sitting favours I could ask for from family and friends, and with doggy day-care not looking a likely option, I decide to advertise for a professional dog-sitter for two afternoons a week.

Writing the advert is tricky. I don't want to be too honest and put off any potential candidates but I also don't want to breach any advertising standards by making false claims. I thought posting on social media was probably the best bet so at least friends knew what they were in for. I'd certainly made no bones about what a nightmare the pups could be. A good friend recommended someone who lived locally and he agreed to come and meet us first thing in the morning. It sounded promising and I tried not to get my hopes up, although inside I was doing a happy dance.

Tuesday 15 January

It is fair to say that Barry was not what I was expecting for a young guy who spent his days walking Weimaraners and cuddling Cockapoos. Buff Barry was as wide as he was short, and covered head to toe in tattoos. However, this was not what surprised me most. What surprised me the most was the fact that he was completely shit-scared of the dogs. Not only was he clueless about what to do while they sniffed and circled him excitedly (stand calmly and ignore them – Ridgebacks are very wary of new people), his voice went up two octaves as he talked nervously to them in what can only be described as a high-octane baby voice. The pups looked as perplexed as I did. His nerves settled slightly once I explained to him that he wouldn't need to walk them, just play with them, and watch them for a few hours while I went out. And he relaxed further when I said that I would stay in today so that he could get used to the pups – which effectively meant that I was paying to sit the dog-sitter! But it was an investment, and I was determined to make it work. The pups needed to be happy with him and he needed to be confident with them. And I needed some time off before I lost my mind.

Saturday 19 January

Now that the pups are six months old, they can be weaned from four meals down to three. This means the colossal food bill should reduce by 25%. I've also decided to switch from raw food to dry food (kibble) for three reasons:

1. it is disgusting and I have to disinfect all surfaces to avoid the spread of e-coli and poisoning the whole family
2. I keep forgetting to take the food out of the freezer the night before and the pups are ready to eat their own limbs for breakfast while it defrosts – which is about the only thing they haven't yet eaten
3. it's ludicrously expensive and their weekly food bill is more than ours

I set off on my mission to find a good quality, reasonably priced kibble at our pet store. After a long search through all the different varieties, weighing up nutritional value versus cost, I come across a well-established brand which is highly recommended by vets. A saving of £10 a bag is a £30 saving a week which could go towards the contents insurance for all the things they've destroyed. I made my way to the till with a little spring in my step.

'You're not givin' 'em THAT, are you?' came a gruff voice from behind me. I was startled at being spoken to in this manner by a member of staff, but she continued, 'It's 'orrible stuff, terrible stuff.'

'I'm just giving it to them for lunch. They'll still have their raw food in the mornings and evenings,' I lied. Why I had to explain myself to this woman was ridiculous.

I hurried out, feeling guilty, but that was only until I watched the pups wolf it down with delight. And the best thing was that one bag lasted three days as opposed to one day for the same price of raw food! Result!

When I got home, I realised I'd forgotten the treats. Gah! I'd left them on the till counter. It was too risky to go back, so I decided to go tomorrow. Hopefully the upstart doesn't work Sundays.

Sunday 20 January

I returned to the pet store to collect the ludicrously overpriced, organic, grain-free dog treats I'd left there yesterday. These are the only fart-free dog biscuits currently on the market and so they're worth every pound.

'You gave 'em that food again yesterday, didn't ya!' came the dulcet tones of the judgey sales assistant. 'Why d'ya do that? I told you it's bad for 'em!'

I was about to spew out some long-winded excuse when I just said, honestly, 'Because I can't afford to spend £100 a week to feed two puppies on top of everything else. This way, I save 30 quid a week, so it's more manageable, and they still have three healthy meals a day.'

'When are they a year?' she snapped.

'In July,' I said through gritted teeth.

'Then you should be giving 'em three raw meals a day until then and not THIS stuff.'

Well, they are not your dogs and it's none of your business. You take my entire earnings every week. I might as well have my bank pay my wage directly into your shop's account. I've cut down on my own food bill. Organic food for the family is now a thing of the past so that I can provide my dogs with non-hide chews, grain-free treats, spirulina and kale teeth-cleaning supplies and a list of other "essentials" that didn't even exist five years ago! I think they'll survive on a vet-recommended diet of high-quality expensive dog food which YOU SELL IN YOUR SHOP. Obviously, on a busy Sunday, I said none of that and instead replied, 'I'll swap it as soon as I can.'

She followed me to the till and said loudly, 'If you're gonna go for the CHEAP food, you should at least go for the one with joint care so they don't get ARTHRITIS.'

I'll find out her day off if it kills me.

Monday 21 January

I'm meeting a friend for shopping and lunch today and can barely contain my excitement. It will be the first time I've gone out by myself for a half-day without worrying about the pups in almost five months. I've booked Barry for four hours. Paying someone to play with the pups feels like money well spent. It means the pups will have someone to give them their undivided attention while I get some me-time. They'll be in heaven playing with someone new, and I'll come home refreshed and invigorated, and hopefully they'll be knocked out from exhaustion.

Barry was due to arrive at 10.00 a.m. I'd factored in a thirty-minute settling-in period, and as Ivan was working from home, Barry wouldn't be left with the dogs by himself. By 10.30 he still hadn't arrived. I called him and he said he was stuck in traffic – which was an unlikely story given that he lived half a mile away. He finally arrived an hour late and looked as nervous as he did the first time he was here. He jumped out of his skin when the pups greeted him. Interestingly, they didn't jump up but encircled him like a shark circling its prey. I told him to relax and that the dogs would be fine, but he was jittery and wittering on in a manic voice which was beginning to excite the pups and irritate me. Ivan came downstairs and introduced himself, and reassured Barry that he would be working from home should he need anything. Barry looked hugely relieved. I told Barry to make sure they do a wee before putting them in their crates when he leaves, and I demonstrated how obedient they are when given their instructions to do a wee and go to bed. I was running late so told him to ask Ivan if he needed anything else. I left him with a worried look on his face and two dogs staring at him expectantly. I was only going to be gone a few hours for goodness' sake, and he is supposed to be used to dogs given that he's a dog-sitter.

Before I came home, I'd had a dozen Instagram-worthy photographs of the dogs sent to me by Barry. The last one was an action photo of Otis mid-stream doing a wee, presumably to prove that he had followed my instruction. Ivan had also sent me a message during lunch which said, 'Barry's constant out-of-tune whistling is driving me up the flipping wall. I feel sorry for the dogs.'

But needs must, and as sitters aren't exactly queuing up right now, I felt grateful that someone was willing to do this job, even if they were rubbish.

Tuesday 22 January

I've got to get our tax returns done ASAP and need something to keep the pups amused during the afternoon so I can concentrate. Since Ridgebacks are intelligent, I have invested in a new batch of puzzle toys where I can hide treats inside them and they have to use their problem-solving skills to get them out. As they love food more than life itself, I am confident this toy will be a hit, despite the fact that puppies generally have the attention span of a midge. Kiara has a purple rubber hive with weird shapes cut out of it where I can squeeze the treats in, and Otis has a long phallic toy shaped like a blue cucumber with similar cut outs. I was grateful these were delivered by Amazon and that I didn't have to purchase them in person.

I stuffed the toys with treats and gave them one each. Unbelievably, they were so excited, they didn't even fight over each other's and rushed off to figure them out. It took Otis approximately half a second to get his out before he tried to take Kiara's off her. However, she warned him off with a menacing growl I'd not heard before, and he stood watching her as she used her teeth and claws to try and get the treats out. After a few minutes, she tossed it in the air in frustration and gave up. I helped her by pushing them out a little bit but Otis snuck in, grabbed it and ran out into the garden with it. Instead, I gave Kiara a new toy which Ella had chosen which we were saving for later in the week. Timmy Twisty Legs was a heavy-duty toy for large dogs with bone-breaking jaws. Within minutes, poor Timmy had suffered the same fate as his other "indestructible" friends and had been decapitated, amputated, disembowelled and squeaker removed. I actually felt sorry for him. Otis came in and grabbed the once safely embedded squeaker, AKA choking hazard, in his mouth and squeaked it manically while Kiara finished off Timmy's remains.

I got one page of accounts done and am back to the drawing board regarding dog distraction plans.

Wednesday 23 January

Barry turned up forty-five minutes late and wearing headphones which he didn't remove until I suggested he did so. For this week's dog-sitting session, I proposed that Barry take Otis for a short walk around the block to break the boredom for all concerned. After he'd got over the initial shock and I had assured him that Otis was fine on lead, he set off. I confess that I did spy on him by driving down the road a few minutes later, only to see Otis being practically strangled by such a short lead as Barry was gripping onto it for dear life and pulling it taut from nerves. I made a mental note to scrap the walk in future. Boredom is preferable to strangulation, I decided.

I went to the supermarket and received the usual barrage of photos, including some of the pups "playing" in the garden which involved them sleeping on the trampoline and lying down next to a ball. It was strange, but they just weren't interested in playing with Barry and I had no idea why. Well, I did have my suspicions.

Thursday 24 January

Ella's friend came over after school. She has got used to the dogs now and especially loves Kiara, particularly when she's asleep and she's all soft and cuddly. I also like Kiara when she's asleep but for different reasons. The three of us took Otis out for a walk. I'd forgotten that walking a dog can actually be an enjoyable experience as opposed to a stressful affair, risking life and limb. We played his favourite game, where Ella runs to the other end of the field while I hold him back and then when I let him go, he races at full speed to catch her. I then run in the opposite direction and he chases me. It's a great way for us all to get exercise. I explained to Ella's friend that when a large dog charges towards you at speed, you must stand absolutely still. Although it may look like he's going to run straight into you and break every bone in your body, he will only do this if you move out of the way at the last second. I suggested that if she was scared, then it was best to either shut her eyes or face the other way. She found the best way was to stand behind Ella, and scream like a banshee. Otis skims so close when he does this that you can feel the wind as he goes past. Seeing him run at full speed is awesome to watch. A bit scary but awesome all the same. Strength, agility, muscle and speed. And the amazing thing is that he doesn't get slower the bigger he gets, he gets faster.

Friday 25 January

Today when Barry came over both pups went straight to bed. Barry texted me several times to tell me that they wouldn't come out of their beds. I gave advice on how to encourage them to come out and play, something I never thought I'd hear myself say, but they still wouldn't come out. This was extremely unusual and I worried there might be something wrong with them. Maybe they were sick? I came home early, paid Barry and agreed to see him next week. The moment the door shut, Otis and Kiara came out of their beds and ran around like their usual loony selves.

Thursday 31 January

I took Otis for his walk to our favourite spot at the hotel. I parked outside the hotel in a guest spot and thought it would be nice to do a lap of the front gardens before going down to the lake at the back.

A disgruntled man came out of the hotel and approached me, asking what I was doing walking my dog in the grounds. I was about to ask what business it was of his when I glanced at his badge – the Hotel Manager. Shit! I pondered putting on a Spanish accent and pretending I didn't speak English, but at the last second I decided not to which was a very good idea as the hotel manager was in fact, Spanish.

'You are not allowed to walk your dog here!' he said, correctly as would have it. There was a large sign right behind his head. 'We've put up signs so that people don't walk their dogs here, so you are trespassing.' He was not muchos happy.

'Do you live here?' he asked accusingly. I took a quick

glance at the tiny townhouses on the right which weren't big enough to swing a cat in let alone a grown dog, and said, 'Yes, I live just over there,' pointing in their direction.

'Then you should walk it in YOUR garden,' he said. 'Now LEAVE!' he shouted, which made Otis and me both jump. 'I am the manager of this hotel and if you don't leave, I am calling the police'.

The problem with this situation was that my car was right behind him, at the hotel entrance, and my fictitious house was across the green in the opposite direction. He stood there defiantly and I had no choice but to walk towards my pretend abode. I flounced off as he watched, scowling, with arms folded, praying he would go back into the hotel, but he didn't budge. He knew I didn't live here and it was totally humiliating. I continued towards the houses then did a quick 180 and ran across the green in the direction of my car. Unbelievably, he started chasing me! He was absolutely livid. Otis didn't have the foggiest idea what was going on but sensed my panic and shot into the car like an arrow. As I screeched back in reverse, he took out his phone and started filming me, running along beside my car. 'Are you fucking SERIOUS?' Now I was furious.

I made sure all the doors were locked before opening my window and yelling, 'Tell YouTube I said hi. You maniac!' and I sped off.

Otis was distressed by all the shouting but I was hoping to God that video didn't go viral or we'd never find anywhere to trespass ever again.

CHAPTER 7 – FEBRUARY

NEIGHBOUR ALIENATION

Saturday 2 February

Finding a new place to walk Otis shouldn't be too difficult, finding one for Kiara is another matter. I have to concede – I have no control over this dog whatsoever. My theory now is, if I can't control *her*, then I will control her environment instead. This means finding a place to walk Kiara where there are no dogs and preferably no people. The only place I can think of with no people – live ones anyway – is the cemetery, and as luck would have it, there's one just around the corner from us.

I got up early to try it out before anyone was up. I can't say I'm a big fan of cemeteries but on this bright morning it looks serene and beautiful. It's lovingly kept and more importantly, has several pathways forking off if I need to make a sharp pivot should someone decide to visit a loved one before sunrise.

Unfortunately, the cliché of crows flocking to cemeteries is true, and every time Kiara sees one, she yanks my arm out of its socket, pulling the lead taut and barking furiously until they fly away. Crows are masochists and come back immediately to taunt Kiara. It's exhausting and not the calm walk I expected at 6 a.m. on a Saturday morning. The only thing that could make it worse is if the miserable old git with his two greyhounds in matching coats comes in. They hate Kiara. As I turn the corner, the miserable git with his two greyhounds in matching tartan coats appears. I call it a day and run back to the car before another calamity results.

Curious to find out why there are so many crows in the cemetery, I look it up. It says it's because there are ample bugs and worms crawling out of the ground for them to feast on. It puts me right off my breakfast.

Monday 4 February

Barry was coming over to dog-sit and I was racking my brains to find a polite way to end this pointless gig without offending him. It was clear the dogs hadn't bonded with him which Ivan thought might be due to his tuneless whistling. Everyone whistles out of tune when wearing headphones, which made me wonder whether this was also part of the reason they hadn't bonded. You have to be mentally as well as physically present when looking after dogs. They know if someone genuinely cares about them or whether they're just doing it for the money. Ivan thought perhaps he was listening to podcasts on how to get over the fear of dogs. Barry was a sweet guy, but if the dogs retreated to their crates whenever he came over then I might as well put them in there, go out and forfeit the dog-sitting fee.

The pups got all excited when they heard a car in the driveway but when they clocked Barry, they both went to bed. Otis even feigned snoring. I took a deep breath and readied myself for the final goodbye when Barry told me he had some bad news. He was regrettably quitting dog-sitting as he'd been head-hunted by a recruitment agency for a high-flying tech job that was just too good to turn down. As much as he loved his time with us, sadly this would be his last day. Grateful that I wasn't the one doing the firing, I wished him well on his new path, hopefully without looking too relieved.

That night he posted a photo on Instagram of a new dog he was sitting for – a Shih Tzu in South London called

Lady Caroline. I didn't want to rumble him so I didn't acknowledge the post. It was better to go along with the charade than humiliate him. Besides, I think a Shih Tzu is probably more up his street than my two beasts, and I genuinely did wish him all the best.

So once again, it's me and the pups 24/7. I wonder, if I wear headphones and whistle out of tune whether the pups will go to bed for the day?

Wednesday 6 February

A message from one of the owners on the puppy Facebook Group asked whether the male puppies had dropped both their balls yet as her dog had only dropped one. I peered at Otis's sack and replied, saying that Otis hadn't dropped either ball yet. A barrage of aghast responses telling me to book him in at the vets and have him castrated immediately, worried me. He was only seven months old and wasn't supposed to be "done" until he was fully grown at two years. The lady who'd posted the message then texted me a close-up photo of her dog's one bollock! After the initial shock, I burst out laughing, relieved, replying that Otis had in fact dropped both balls, I just didn't realise they were supposed to look like two shiny ripe kiwis. I contemplated sending a pic of Otis's balls to show my error, but felt this was a vast invasion of his privacy. Plus, I didn't want to get arrested for sending dick pics of my dog. They would just have to take my word for it. I deleted the photo of her dog's testicle off my phone as it would have been difficult to explain it away should anyone stumble across it.

Thursday 7 February

I've found a secret spot to walk Kiara where we won't bump into a single soul and which doesn't involve me skulking around a cemetery at the crack of dawn like a weirdo. There's a dirt track behind Ella's school that runs around the sports grounds all the way to the staff car park. It's perfect. It means I have to wait until all the parents have dropped off their kids before I sneak in but it's worth the wait. When the last mother finally stops gossiping and leaves, I drive to the far end of the pupil car park and climb under the railings with Kiara.

Without anyone around I can practise training Kiara to "heel" or at least walk without her going demented when she spots another creature. She is relatively calm and even the odd squirrel doesn't faze her. I'm so relieved. She won't do a poo when she's on the lead and I'm tempted to let her off, but I resist the temptation as I'm not a complete fool (just a partial one). As we reach the end of the path, I turn and am facing head-on into the headmistress's office window. I'm not sure whether to duck or wave. Luckily, she's busy working and doesn't spot me, so I duck down and creep along the path behind the bushes until we're out of sight. I make a mental note not to walk that far in future. I'm not going to blow this ideal walking spot and may have to consider camouflage attire just to be sure. This place is worth its weight in gold.

Friday 8 February

A greatly anticipated mums' night out results in me waxing lyrical about the nightmare that is currently my life. Much to everyone's hilarity (I must admit it did sound funny with the pups safely at home and a few Pinot Grigios under my belt), I did discover several helpful realisations:

1. the fantasy of me strutting down the street with two obedient dogs by my side is a pipe dream
2. these are African lion hunters and their pack instinct is always going to be stronger than my rationale (which basically means they'll never listen to me when they're together)
3. getting a large dog who's stronger than me was optimistic, getting two was idiotic
4. Kiara is definitely nuts

Saturday 9 February

My Aunt is over from Canada and is keen to meet the pups. After being licked and mauled she is even more keen to get out of here and take Ella to Madame Tussauds, despite the three-hour queues. Although I'd like to collapse on the sofa and eat crisps all day, I am going to make use of a free Saturday and take the pups for a walk in the big boys playground – Richmond Park. This is quite a leap from their usual outings, but if you don't try, you'll never know.

I took Otis first and when the coast was clear, i.e., no deer or dogs in sight, I let him off the lead for a bit. I half-expected him to run off and herd deer but he stayed right next to me for almost the entire time. He did terrorise a couple of rabbits by chasing them down a hole, but other than that, it was most definitely a success. Although curious about the deer, he was too petrified to actually approach one.

I took Kiara, and returned a hot mess. She is most definitely NOT ready to walk in Richmond Park now or probably ever. I kept her on lead and spent the entire time being yanked from tree to tree as she played Whack-A-Mole with every squirrel she saw. I steered clear of the deer but when we came across a stag, she honestly thought she could take this giant beast down. It took all my strength to hold her back. Even a cold stare from the beautiful but intimidating giant didn't throw her. This dog has kamikaze tendencies and I did not feel safe for me, her or even the stag. Throughout all this, I miraculously managed to keep my cool and used my firm, but not raised, voice until we got back to the car where I used my hysterical voice. As I was clipping Kiara's seatbelt onto her harness, she slid past me and bolted out of the car towards a group of mums and their toddlers. The screams could be heard in Central London.

When I finally caught her, I was panting more heavily than she was. That dog has no fear, no boundaries and the speed and strength of Popeye. I need to up my game. And I need to keep her on her lead until she is bolted into her seatbelt.

Ella came home from a fun day out, holding a creepy wax mould of her hand which I could see Kiara had her watchful eye on. She'd also bought me a mini Oscar statue which said Best Mum Ever. It's good to know I'm doing at least one job properly.

Tuesday 12 February

Unfortunately, Jane has lost her job. Fortunately for me, it means she's available for regular dog-sitting until she finds another one. Jane adores the pups and happily accepts my offer of two afternoons a week. I'm off to Kingston for some retail therapy and to pick up some bits for Ella's school play.

The pups were overjoyed when Jane arrived. She wore her special dog clothes which are essentially items of clothing which she doesn't mind getting "worn in", as she politely puts it. Otis jumped up, ripping a tear into Jane's jacket before she'd even taken her shoes off. Talking of which, she wisely remembered to lock those away in Ella's room.

Glancing in the car mirror, I looked like I'd aged a decade. A well-deserved trip to the makeup counter was definitely on the cards today although there wasn't enough concealer in the entire makeup department of John Lewis to disguise my eye bags. Plastic surgery was a more realistic option.

I finished the day with a browse in the dog section at TK Maxx and found all sorts of toys and bedding for the pups. It dawned on me that even when I wasn't with the dogs, I was thinking about them. It was like they were becoming part of my DNA and I thought about their needs almost as much as I did Ella's (although her needs were a piece of cake in comparison). I stocked up on as much as I could carry and headed home.

'I'm completely exhausted,' Jane said as I stepped through the door. 'I don't know how you do it full time. Just keeping an eye on them for a few hours and I need a lie down and I didn't have to do anything else! I applaud you,' she said, genuinely impressed. And admittedly, she did look completely knackered.

Trying to keep the desperation out of my voice, I asked, 'Are you still happy to look after them?'

'Oh yes, but maybe just for two or three hours next time. Four hours was a little much.'

'Deal,' I said. I'll take whatever I can get.

Wednesday 13 February

It's the second week of walking Kiara behind Ella's school. She is doing so well, I can't quite believe it. Without any environmental stressors like people, pets, wildlife, cars or mobility scooters, she is really calm and actually listens to me. I've taken a slightly longer lead today so she has a few extra metres to roam and I can practise her recall. Even if she comes back to me 10% of the time it will be progress. Actually, a turn of her head to acknowledge I'm speaking to her will be an improvement. I have new treats to reward her and miraculously it's working. We do three tries at recall and she stops walking and comes back to me every time. 'Good girl, Kiara,' I say, and I'm almost in tears I'm so happy. Excited by my exuberant praise, she winds herself in and out of my legs. Just as I'm about to make the lead a bit longer, I hear a loud whistle in the distance and see an early sports practice is about to start. I clock the scary PE teacher before she spots me, crouch down and creep back to the car. Better to cut the walk short while making great progress anyway, I thought. I gave Kiara a mountain of treats for her good behaviour and left with hope in my heart.

Thursday 14 February

I was hoovering mud off the living-room floor for the third time today when I heard the pups barking at the end of the garden. It was the neighbour's dog again. That little mutt spends his life winding up my dogs by standing at the fence and barking at them. He does this, safe in the knowledge that there is a barrier protecting him so he can be as bolshie as he likes. I waited for the pups to get bored and come back in but they didn't. With all three of them still at it, I went into the garden and called Otis and Kiara back indoors. Nothing. Otis always comes back when he's called, but he didn't even poke his head around the tree this time. I grabbed my flip-flops and made my way down the garden, calling them more sternly. The barking was in full flow but they were nowhere to be seen. My stomach flipped and the blood drained from my face as I realised, with horror, they'd escaped. They'd got into the neighbour's garden. The neighbour with the prize flower bed. The neighbour who hates us. I ran to the end of the garden and sure enough, there were two big black noses poking up at me from over the stretch of four-foot fence along the side of our garden. Of course, they couldn't get back over the fence they'd had no trouble clearing ten minutes earlier when they'd decided to trespass. I yelled out to Ivan who came hurtling down the garden. He clambered over the fence, picked them up and threw them back over. My only saving grace was that no one was home to witness it.

Ten minutes later the doorbell rang. Ivan opened the door and there stood the irate neighbour who on a scale of 1 to 10 of wanting to kill us, was an 11. I hid in the laundry room as she proceeded to spit out that our dogs were out of control and had ripped up the chicken wire on her flower bed and dug up her prize-winning flowers. They'd terrorised her dog and barked at her incessantly when she tried to shoo them away whilst on an important work call. They then chased each other around the garden for the next twenty minutes (which was a slight exaggeration but I wasn't about to interject). Ivan apologised profusely, offering to pay for any damage and promised to put up sturdy fencing in the morning. And shoot the dogs (joke – obviously! Although I think she would have liked to).

Friday 15 February

Pre-breakfast run around the garden with the pups under strict surveillance so that they didn't jump into the neighbour's garden before the new fencing was erected. It was a freezing cold morning with a gale-force wind. I was wearing my old boots and dressing gown which was flapping around whilst trying to pick up a colossal dog poo and keeping an eye on them both. After they were tired out, we came back in and I headed off for a shower. For once, I was left alone in the bathroom without them nicking things out of the bin, dragging the towels off the rail and licking the soap on the trays. Which meant something was up…

I quickly towelled myself off and called them but there was no sound of their scurrying paws. I sprinted into the kitchen to see the patio doors wide open. How the hell had they let themselves out when I'd locked the doors! Frantically calling them, I threw on my dressing gown and boots and shot down the garden, semi-naked. Otis appeared from behind the trees but Kiara was nowhere in sight. I scrambled over the fence and there she was, running around the neighbour's garden, making a complete spectacle of herself. The entire family and their dog were lined up along their French doors watching me while I ran around hopelessly trying to catch her, my dressing gown flapping open and me trying desperately not to expose myself! It was mortifying. I didn't know whether to laugh or cry as all five of them watched on with stern faces. Just as I caught the little shit, she jumped up and smacked me in the mouth, splitting my lip. As my mouth filled with blood, I gripped her tightly and dropped her into our garden. As I ungraciously straddled the now rickety fence, I scraped all down the inside of my thigh and ripped back a finger nail. I stormed into the house, shut them in their crates and got dressed as quickly as possible so I could take Ella to school before the neighbour appeared at our door again.

Bleeding, sore and humiliated, I waited for the knock at the door, or the irate text, but there was nothing, which was worse. I had a magnesium salt bath to soothe my sore muscles, forgetting I was covered in scratches and grazes

– it was like being dipped into a bath of vinegar, it was so painful. But it was nothing compared to the pain I was feeling inside.

Saturday 16 February

Ella is the lead in her school play, which requires a lot of to-ing and fro-ing from school for rehearsals. It makes sense to walk Kiara in our secret spot when I drop Ella off, so I bring her with us in the car.

Kiara is a nightmare in the car. She has a deafening bark which she uses to full effect when spotting anything that so much as moves outside the car. Short of blacking out the entire car windows or shooting her with a tranquilizer gun, I have resorted to the distraction method of sprinkling stinky salmon treats all over the back seat. Unfortunately, all treats are devoured before I've even reversed out of the drive so I stopped off at the pet store to buy the longest, toughest chew they sell. The sales girl assured me that her Boxer takes four hours to get through one of these chews. This equates to an estimated thirty minutes with Kiara's jaws. It takes Kiara just under two minutes to devour this chew before she is sitting back up at the window, slobbering and barking at every twig that sways, every leaf that falls, every traffic light that changes and human and non-human animal we pass. Ella is in tears at the ear-splitting bark of this mad dog. I am going to have to invest in industrial ear plugs for any trips in future or maybe a blindfold for Kiara.

Monday 18 February

It's an unusually mild day and Ella is wearing her fluffy earmuffs on the drive to school. I realise it's to block out the sound of Kiara's barking. But while training is going so well in the school grounds, I am reluctant to give this up, and conclude this is not a bad idea and deliberate wearing some myself.

Sadly, the earmuffs will not be needed for the mornings in future. Our secret walking spot has now been scuppered by over-zealous sporty girls who'd rather spend their early mornings practising hockey than having an extra fifteen minutes in bed like a normal child. The screaming and shouting from the girls, and incessant blowing of the whistle, is turning both Kiara and myself into nervous wrecks. And ducking and diving to avoid being spotted through the hedgerow is adding to the stress. Oh well, it was good while it lasted. It's back to the drawing board and back on the lookout for more places to trespass to walk my crazy pup.

Wednesday 20 February

I was called into school early to collect Ella as she'd been sick at lunch time. The drama teacher looked close to a nervous breakdown as it's the school production tomorrow night and there is no understudy. I assured her that Ella would be fine by tomorrow and that it was probably just nerves.

Poor Ella looked as white as a ghost when I picked her up. She laid on the sofa with a blanket which she shared with the pups. They were so overjoyed to have her home that they both cuddled up to her and went to sleep for the entire afternoon. Even crazy pups have a sixth sense when humans are poorly. I'm keeping my fingers crossed Ella will be okay by the morning. A Robin Hood musical doesn't really work without Robin Hood in it.

Thursday 21 February

Although Ella is looking a bit pasty, she is determined to make it in for the show. School have given her the day off to get her strength back so she can go in for the performance tonight. Otis and Kiara approve of this decision and spend the day watching movies with her. When an advert comes on with a dog barking, Kiara runs straight down the garden to investigate where this dog is, while Otis watches her, confused. With the new fencing still not up, I race after her and bring her back inside, muting the television whenever a dog appears on the screen. I literally never get a moment's peace.

After an amazing show I'm beaming at how proud I am of Ella to give such a great performance whilst clearly feeling like death. This is the first night the pups have been left on their own, but as they were in their crates, the house was still in the same condition we left it in. Even Ridgebacks can't chew their way out of steel. They went bonkers when they saw us. I think they thought we weren't coming home. The thought never crossed my mind.

Saturday 23 February

As I'm running out of places to walk Kiara in the UK, I took her to our old stomping ground where I first used to walk them, hoping this would be a familiar and stress-free environment. The park was deserted and it seemed tiny now they were bigger. It was barely light and even the birds were still asleep. The park had become a swamp from the recent monsoon-like rains and it took all my effort not to slip arse over tit. Kiara had no trouble navigating this danger zone in her ninja style. As I trundled along the slippery path, I kept a lookout for any potential dog-walkers in the distance. You can never be too sure, even at this ridiculous hour. I was beginning to suss out that there were others out there like Kiara, who also needed to be walked at unsociable hours to avoid normal life. It was all clear, or so I thought. But Kiara, with her bionic eyesight, spotted a speck of black fluff on the horizon. As adrenalin surged through her and her fight-or-flight instinct took over, her 30 kilos swiftly turned into 60 kilos of strength, and it was not humanly possible to stop her from taking off. The lead whipped through my hands, leaving rope burns as she went. She disappeared over the horizon in seconds. I ran after her as fast as I could in a giant sludge pit, following the direction of her barking. As I caught up to her, panting and heaving, I saw a well dressed middle-aged woman standing there, with a big shaggy black dog by her side. The dog stood perfectly still as Kiara ran around them, barking like a maniac. I apologised profusely as I tried to grab her. I was so embarrassed both by her behaviour and the fact that I couldn't catch her, that I blurted out that Kiara was a rescue dog. This was met with what I could only interpret as complete and utter contempt. 'She's really scared and is just protecting us,' I desperately added. But the woman was having none of it.

'*My* dog is a rescue dog,' she said pointedly whilst staring me down. 'And she is *blind*.'

I was stumped. There was no comeback after that. I am definitely going to hell. At least I'll have Kiara for company.

Sunday 24 February

There's nothing like depressing yourself with a quick look at #dogsofinstagram.

Whilst a normal forty-something-year-old woman would be admiring the looks and styles of trendy fashion influencers, I instead am fantasising about having puppies who are not social lepers.

I came across a vegan activist and all-round babe feeding her perfect little sausage dog with a vegan dog meal. Feeling like a hypocrite every time I fill the family food trolley with animal-free products and then packing the boot of my car with the pups' dog food of dead animals, I decided to give it a try. Maybe some Zen-like nutrition might calm them down a bit. They say you are what you eat, in which case they must be eating feral ferrets.

I go to my lovely new upmarket pet store (where I will never bump into that other twerp) and ask them if they have any vegan dog food, presuming the response to be a loud guffaw followed by a hard, no. Unbelievably, they say yes! With exuberance, they show me the packet, which looks legit, and then warn me that it's not quite vegan because it's actually insects. My face must have mirrored what I was thinking, which was, you think a Rhodesian Ridgeback is going to be satisfied with a plate of ants and spiders for dinner? They are currently having three large meals daily and still scavenging for scraps every waking hour of the day. But when they show me the high protein content, the vast number of nutrients and its low carbon footprint, I'm sold. I am shocked at how environmentally unfriendly it is owning a dog. Feeding a dog meat is responsible for a considerable percentage of carbon emissions! Man's best friend certainly isn't Mother Nature's best friend, and I need to do my bit to help.

I buy two 6 kilo bags and vow to give it a go, but my gut instinct is that it ain't gonna go down well. I pour the dead insects into the pups' bowls with a little too much gusto to get them enthused, but to my astonishment, they wolf it down. Mother Nature and her animals will be pleased. The insects not so much. I did feel guilty about that, but consoled myself that they only live a few days, I think.

Later that night, the noxious gasses emanating from Otis and Kiara were like nothing I have ever smelt before in my life. And I used to work in the ICU at an animal sanctuary so I know the smell of a roomful of hot shit first thing in the morning. I've changed plenty of stinky nappies too but that was NOTHING compared to this!

I opened all the windows in the living room, the patio doors and then the rest of the doors in the house. I would have taken the roof off if I could. It was nuclear. Silent but deadly had never been so apt. Even the pups were wondering where on earth the smell was coming from. With cotton wool stuffed up both nostrils, I couldn't concentrate on my movie and called it a night.

The next morning Ella and Ivan both asked, 'What is that stench?'

I won't be buying that food again, but I will keep what's left in the cupboard should someone come over who I want to get rid of. The search for sustainable, cruelty-free food continues.

Tuesday 26 February

Finally, the fencing arrived! I text the neighbours with the good news. Ivan is putting it up later and as a precaution, I am taking the pups into the garden separately, on lead, until then. I cannot take any chances. I take Otis into the garden first as he needs to wee for Britain when he wakes up. As I carefully slide the patio door open, Kiara, appearing from nowhere, knocks him out the way, pushes past me and hares down to the end of the garden.

Two irate phone calls later and the neighbours are threatening to take us to court. I'm facing the threat of either a fine or prosecution, but secretly hoping that the dog will be taken away instead.

Tomorrow I will start looking for a new place to live. Preferably a farmhouse in the middle of nowhere where the nearest neighbour lives 50 miles away.

CHAPTER 8 – MARCH

WOMAN ON THE VERGE OF A NERVOUS BREAKDOWN

Friday 1 March

I booked a viewing at a newly refurbished farmhouse near Ella's school. Apart from the neighbour's looming prosecution, our once beautiful garden is now a giant mud pit. Two fast-growing pups hurtling around at breakneck speed means mounds of grass getting ripped up daily. Add in the relentless rain, and there you have the perfect dog-wrestling mud pit.

The farmhouse is a far more suitable option and has land that could be sectioned off just for the pups. It's also the perfect place to eventually have an animal sanctuary – my lifelong dream. With ten acres of land, two barns and only a ten-minute drive from school, it was perfect. The only hiccup was that it was out of our budget and I hadn't told Ivan. This might pose a problem, given that we'd have to sell our house, and rob countless post offices to cover the remainder, but it didn't hurt to have a look. I could always set up a Crowd Funding page for residents down our street as I'm pretty sure most of them would be pleased to see the back of us.

Ella and I completely fell in love with the farmhouse and have already picked out our bedrooms! The layout, the décor, the Feng Shui – everything was perfect. I took a video of the grounds to show Ivan while Ella ran around excitedly discovering all the hidden coves. There was a gorgeous snug area with a hidden staircase leading to Ella's new bedroom.

'This could be your own little hangout space with your friends,' I said.

'And if the dogs weren't allowed in here, I could have a cat,' Ella suggested hopefully. 'Or a rescue pig called Harry Trotter,' she beamed. I didn't mention that rescued animals would need a calm place to recuperate which would mean being as far away from the dogs as possible.

I looked out of the kitchen window (complete with open fireplace – sigh) and imagined the pups tearing about the place. I envisioned fields full of rescued animals and a house full of abandoned pets, and despite the additional mayhem this would bring into our lives, my heart sang. Perhaps having Otis and Kiara was training for my future life. I just had to come up with a way of raising a couple of million quid.

Saturday 2 March

Bright, crisp mornings like these are every dog-walker's dream. I smile as I watch Otis trot along just a few feet in front of me, continually checking to see if I'm still behind him. Just a snap of a twig and he runs up to check that I'm alright. He's such a sensitive soul. I could be face down in a ditch with two broken legs for half an hour before Kiara would even notice. As his glossy coat glistens in the sun, my heart swells at the pure joy this pup brings me.

After the relaxing walk, I was in the kitchen on the phone to my mum when I looked out of the window and saw a Ridgeback puppy staring back at me! There, standing in the driveway with the gates open onto the road, was Otis. I rushed out of the kitchen and saw the front door had blown wide open. Kiara was halfway down the road, chasing the postman, who was running for his life with his trolley at full speed. Otis had now joined the chase. I was calling them both, but to no avail. I ran after them, hurling my arms around to stop traffic whilst the neighbours came out to watch. Otis and Kiara caught up with the postman and circled him, barking in a frenzy. I yelled at the postman to just stand still but he was jumping around, completely petrified, and the dogs thought it was a game. I caught up with Kiara but she kept bolting every time I got near her, and Otis kept slipping out of my grip. Trying to catch two mad dogs, calm the postman down and stop us all being killed from oncoming traffic was as stressful as hell. I was terrified one of the dogs was going to run off and get killed on the main road. As a queue of traffic built up down our road, a woman got out of her car with a slipknot rope and caught Otis, which gave me just enough time to grab Kiara and get them back inside. I was shaking. The pups were shaking. The postman was shaking. I apologised profusely for their behaviour but he was having none of it. It could have ended in disaster and I was just relieved that no one had got hurt, but he was livid. I was pretty sure there wouldn't be any post being delivered any time soon. And I had a bad feeling that this wasn't the last we'd heard of it.

Monday 4 March

There was a knock at the door early this morning. It was the postman. I was fairly certain he wasn't making a special delivery.

'I'm going to have to report you for Saturday's incident,' he said.

'I'm so sorry. I promise it will never happen again. They're actually really friendly once you get to know them. Do you want to come in and meet them?'

'No thank you. It says in our Health & Safety guidelines that we have to report any circumstances where a staff member could be in danger.' He was serious.

'OK,' I said, defeated. 'What happens next?'

'You'll be hearing from my superior,' he said.

Oh God! I shut the door, worried. 'Does this mean we're going to be prosecuted by Royal Mail too?' I asked Ivan.

'Probably,' he said, in his usual comforting manner.

I looked up "prosecutions for dogs chasing postmen down the street" and fortunately there were none. There were, however, lots of prosecutions for dogs who've attacked and bitten postmen leaving them seriously injured. I was astounded at the statistics of dog attacks. An average of 44 postmen and women get attacked by dogs in the UK every week! I can understand now why he was so concerned. One postman was recently knocked down by a dog and broke a hip while the dog continued attacking him! The owner was nowhere to be seen! At least my dogs weren't dangerous. Just crazy.

Tuesday 5 March – Shrove Tuesday (aka Pancake Day)

I walked Otis around the block this morning. The postman saw me and I waved hello. He ignored me and crossed the street. He's probably dumped our mail in the bins behind the flats. I haven't heard from his boss yet and am keeping my fingers crossed it will all blow over.

Ella's twin friends come over after school and I teach them to make pancakes. I lock the dogs in their crates as H is terrified of them. She was scared of our kitten, so I'm not even going to attempt to introduce the pups now they are so big. As the girls come over every Tuesday, I may have to try and find a way of gradually introducing them once they calm down a bit. But for now, I shut the pups in the kitchen with me until home time.

When their dad comes to collect them, there is only one of H's new school shoes by the front door. I try not to show the creeping dread I'm feeling and we all look around the house to find it, although I have a pretty good idea where it is. I grab a torch and head into the garden. It's dark and pouring with rain. I see what's left of a shiny little black shoe on the grass and am mortified. Kids shoes ain't cheap and their dad is not impressed. I offer to pay for a new pair as H is close to tears, worried that she now has to wear trainers to assembly in the morning. I console her as much as I can but am baffled at how and when the pups managed to get the shoe when they'd been with me in the kitchen the entire time. Houdini would be outwitted by these two. From now on, I will make sure all guests shoes are locked away in a cupboard with a combination lock.

Thursday 7 March – World Book Day

Ella is going to school as Olivia from *My Sister the Vampire*. I've added a ponytail extension to her hair and the pups are eyeing it curiously. She flicks her long ponytail at the dogs and I suggest that's probably not the best idea. Kiara's eyes are wide with excitement. That extension wasn't cheap and wouldn't last a second in her clutches, and if a few cotton threads can strangle a dog's insides, I dread to think what an entire Arianna Grande fake ponytail could do.

Saturday 9 March

I'm running the school Movie Night event and load the car up with enough sugary snacks to bring the dead back to life. I need Ivan to set up the projector as I'm a technical Luddite, so my dad has offered to look after the pups. I've bought him a couple of bottles of his favourite Rioja as a thank you. Hopefully, he won't need both bottles this afternoon.

The event went well and we came home with a car full of helium balloons in the characters of Beauty and the Beast, and a child hyped up on enough sugar to stay awake for a week. The pups gave us our usual manic greeting until they saw the balloons and hid behind the sofa. The Beast did look a bit creepy. It was then I noticed that Ella's bedroom door was open a crack.

'All okay?' I asked my dad.

'Yes, they were fine. Otis slept next to me most of the afternoon,' he said.

I didn't need to ask where Kiara had been for the afternoon. I pushed open the door to Ella's bedroom, took a deep breath and closed it again.

The dreamcatcher from Fun Auntie Lisa – which had travelled all the way from Thailand without any damage – was chewed BAR. Same for the pencil case, the birthday spa kit, the sandals, slippers and the crocheted bag. The only things still intact were the bed and the light and that was only because it was fitted to the ceiling.

I gave Ella dinner and cleared away as much of the evidence as possible. I didn't want to spoil her day. I would try and replace as much of it as I could. Thank god for online shopping.

'Mummy, Kiara's lips are blue,' Ella called out.

I opened Kiara's mouth and her tongue was also blue. A cartridge-pen sort of blue.

The white rug under the table also had a large inky-blue patch and underneath the rug was an empty packet of ink cartridges. I couldn't see where the cartridges were, presumably in Kiara's belly. Fortunately, as Ella is on a school trip most of next week, she won't be needing them. I spent the rest of the evening on Amazon trying to replace as many of the chewed items as possible whilst waiting for blue vomit to appear.

Monday 11 March

Ella is away for three nights on a school trip to the Norfolk Lakes and it's forecast to rain for the entire trip. I wave Ella off as she gets on the coach and leave, feeling emotional. The pups cheer me up with their enthusiastic welcome when I walk through the door. I've only been gone for half an hour and they greet me like I've been gone for a week. I marvel at the fact that dogs only have one mood: happy. Happy to see you, happy to play, happy to eat, happy to go out, happy to get up, happy to go to bed. Just happy, always. The only time they're not happy is if they're sick and, touch wood, the pups rarely have anything wrong with them, regardless of the objects consumed daily. Something to say about the robustness of large dogs at least, and the fact that we keep nothing toxic in the house. I say "outside" to the pups and they take off, skidding around the corner to beat each other out the door. They chase each other around the trees, looking back to check I'm watching them. Nothing excites them more than an audience. I hide when they're not looking and we spend the rest of the morning playing their favourite game of hide-and-seek until we're all completely knackered.

Tuesday 12 March

The doorbell rings. Shit, it's the postman. I shut the pups away and open the door wearing the biggest smile I can muster. It is not reciprocated.

'Morning!' I say cheerily. He hands me the parcel and a handful of mail without making eye contact. 'I'm really sorry about the other day. I didn't know you were scared of dogs.'

'I'm not,' he says. 'I have two Huskies.' I was somewhat taken aback by this.

I continued to make small talk and he warmed up slightly. I tested the water and dropped into the conversation that I'd not heard from Royal Mail yet, and he met my eyes and shrugged. I was pretty sure from the look he gave me that he hadn't reported it. Either that or they'd decided dogs playing "it" with the postman didn't warrant sending me to jail. A wave of relief washed over me and I thanked him for the stellar job he was doing. I'm sure I saw a teeny little smile as he turned away.

I logged onto the puppy Facebook Group to see how the others were getting on, expecting to see a load of comments about what a bunch of lunatics they are, but then I remembered I was the only lunatic stupid enough to take two puppies. Today, it was all about the size and weight of the puppies. My two were growing at an alarming rate compared to the others and were the biggest by far. I still wondered whether I was over-feeding them. Even with three meals a day, they act like they're being starved and are constantly on the lookout for scraps on the counter tops or floor. They can hear the crunch of a crisp or the bite of a biscuit from the end of the garden. They have extra-sensory perception when it comes to food, especially human food – basically anything that isn't good for them.

Wednesday 13 March

I can't find the incentive to work today so instead I spend my day checking the school's Twitter feed for photos of the girls on their trip, and searching up holidays to the Caribbean.

Ella's trip looks like a wet weekend, with all the kids standing in the rain identifying pond life in a bucket. Everyone in the Caribbean looks like they've won the lottery and have no intention of ever returning home. I know where I'd rather be. Which gets me thinking… there is nothing we need more right now than a holiday. I find the perfect package deal to Jamaica for Easter. I throw caution to the wind and book it. I text Ivan who is upstairs working and tell him the news. I half expect him to come charging down the stairs, but he texts me back with, 'sounds good!'.

I am beyond excited. A dog-free, stress-free holiday. Heaven! I just have to figure out what to do with the pups while we are away. Who would be willing and mad enough to look after them?

Thursday 14 March

The rain is ricocheting off the kitchen skylight, it's so heavy. Ella is off sick with a temperature, along with half her class after the school trip, and Ivan is in town on a training course. It's dark and dreary and I have two frustrated pups with cabin fever pacing around the house. They are not sure what Ella is doing lying on their sofa during the daytime, and presume she is here to play with them. They continually go in and out of the garden in between the showers, get covered in mud and walk all around the house to ensure no surface is left untouched.

There is an actual puddle in the bathroom where water from the shower has leaked and the pups have trampled their filthy paws in it, creating a muddy puddle to splash around in. Peppa Pig would be proud. There's never any point cleaning when it's raining.

Every time I move they follow me, hoping to be taken for a walk. That's the thing when you have dogs, you can't be a fair-weather walker. They don't get the memo to chill out and miss a walk when it's raining. You have to go whatever the weather. Same with toddlers. I used to take Ella out every day come rain or shine when she was little, but the difference was, she didn't bring half a ton of mud back with her and cover the house with it. She would leave her little welly boots and raincoat at the door and toddle over to the sofa with her sippy cup and watch Peppa Pig. No mess. No fuss. The only muddy puddles we had then were on the television.

As the day went on, the rain became heavier and the wind picked up. By the time Ivan got home, at 3 p.m., the temperature had dropped to four degrees and it was dark. But Otis would not settle until I'd walked him. The woods were out of the question so I reluctantly took him for a windswept walk around the block, the rain lashing into my face. As Otis pulled me around the block, ears flapping in the wind (his, not mine), it was more an exercise in not breaking an ankle as he continually zig-zagged in front of me, tripping me up. Halfway around he did an almighty poo and as I tried to pick it up, the poo bag ripped down one side. I had to walk the rest of the way holding the bag at an angle so the contents didn't fall out whilst the hot stench of dog crap wafted up under my nose, all whilst trying to hold onto 35 kilos of excited wet dog skidding along the lethally slippery pavement. If that isn't love, then I don't know what is. Kiara ran and hid when I called her for a walk. She had no intention of getting wet. Sensible girl. For once.

Sunday 17 March

With the pups' increasing appetite for chewing items other than their toys, the house is looking very orderly. Everything is either in its safe place or eaten. Even the CDs have been taped into their unit so they can't go walkabouts. Although the shoe rack has long since been removed and shoes kept under their respective owner's beds, they somehow still get nabbed and destroyed occasionally. In most households there is the sock Bermuda Triangle. In our house, it's shoes. Two go under the bed, and one comes out. On the advice of my mum, I have started a separate box for the odd shoes which have lost their other halves. This turned out to be a great idea when Kiara ate one of my new Birkenstocks and then ate one from the replacement pair I'd bought. Miraculously, she'd eaten the right shoe from one pair and the left from the other, leaving me with a full pair! I was pretty chuffed about this.

This did not fare so well for Ella's new Lelly Kelly shoes – beautiful silver pumps, intricately sewn with sequins and beads. I buy her a new pair every year. This year they went straight from the box to the bin via the garden where every bead had been pulled off and chewed BAR. Ella was distraught when she spotted the remains in the garden. I assured her we'd buy a new pair straight away, but they'd already sold out. I upped the ante and splashed out on some new swanky boots as a special treat and she was delighted. These boots will not touch the floor unless they are on Ella's feet and will be stored so high up the dogs would need stilts to reach them.

Monday 18 March

My favourite Ray-Bans are missing. I searched high and low and couldn't find them anywhere. My bag, the car, my bedroom…

'Is that them under the table?' Ella asked.

Oh, FFS! On first inspection, they didn't look completely unwearable but when I put them on, neither lens covered my eyes and the arms had been chewed into a point so sharp, they could be classed as a dangerous weapon. I considered wrapping the arms in bubble wrap and securing with Sellotape but then recognised that although my standards were slipping fast, this was a step too far. I was gutted. They were my favourite pair of sunglasses, and a limited edition, but as I'd left them in my handbag on the floor, with dog chews in it, it was my own stupid fault. There was no other option than to just let it go and get over it. This time, it was pretty easy to identify the culprit as the empty chew packet was in Kiara's crate. Either that or Otis was incredibly devious and had eaten the chews and then planted the packet there. But it was getting more apparent that Kiara was the instigator of most of the bad behaviour around here.

Tuesday 19 March

Met up with an old friend, AJ, who wanted me to meet her new puppy. I omitted the fact that I'd had enough of puppies to last me a lifetime and could think of a million other things I'd rather do, like rubbing hot peppers in my eyes. I went to the café to meet her. She had politely asked me not to bring my dogs in case her puppy got frightened as he was still so tiny. I told her not to worry as dog-friendly places did not include my dogs in their description. Besides, I was looking forward to a morning off.

I think "dog-friendly" cafés need to redefine their description to "friendly dog only" cafes because most of the dogs in there couldn't stand each other. Dogs are naturally territorial and although they love hanging out with their owners, they do not particularly like hanging out with a bunch of dogs they don't know in a café, crammed under a table with the smell of freshly cooked muffins wafting around. As AJ stressed out, trying to keep her puppy out of harms reach from the older dogs (by stuffing it into her bag), or eating any stray crumbs off the floor for fear of food poisoning, I, for once, was the most relaxed patron in the place. I ordered myself several freshly baked muffins which I had all to myself without any drooling dogs at my feet. It was bliss. I will make it my mission to now go to dog-friendly cafes on my own without any dogs just to eat muffins and gloat.

Wednesday 20 March

Ella's new friend is coming over for tea after school. She loves dogs and can't wait to meet Ella's two puppies.

I have to shut the pups in the kitchen as it turns out she doesn't like large puppies.

As she's a fussy eater, her mum suggests I give them pizza for tea. I bought some dough and thought it would be fun for them to create their own toppings. The pups thought it would be fun to eat the pizzas before I put them in the oven. I didn't tell the girls, quickly made some replicas and fortunately, they didn't spot the difference. I am expecting double bouts of diarrhoea later as I'm guessing raw dough is probably not good for a dog's digestion.

Thursday 21 March

Now the pups are head height to the counter tops and table, it means I have to make sure nobody leaves anything on them that the dogs could grab. It was hard enough being on keeping-the-floor-clear duty, but now being on keeping-every-surface-clear duty it requires even more vigilance. It's amazing how many things get left on surfaces until you spend your time extracting them from puppies' mouths. Now that the pups have free run of the house, I have to ensure every bedroom door is shut the moment someone leaves their room, the bathroom door is shut after someone uses it and that no one answers the front door without the pups being shut away. Food must be cleared away the second it's finished, and bags, shoes, coats, scarves, etc., are put away and not left dangling anywhere. Homework, rubbers and pencils are not left on the table and oven gloves, heat mats and utensils are not left on the counter tops. Since most of the time the family forget all of the above, I am either constantly nagging them or running around like a blue-arsed fly with a clinical case of OCD. It's exhausting.

I love the pups to bits but this is so much harder than I thought it would be.

Friday 22 March

Barbie is dead. Last week, she lost an arm, yesterday a foot and tonight her head is missing. Ken will be mortified. Ella has ordered a new one on Amazon so hopefully he won't notice.

Saturday 23 March

I took a shower, leaving the pups loose in the house, and was greeted with the usual excitable reception when I got out. The towel and the bathmat stayed clean for a nano-second before being covered in black muddy paw prints. Which was odd because I hadn't let them outside and the patio doors were locked. So, where the hell had this mud come from?

Dripping wet and wrapped in a towel, I ran to the kitchen. They'd fathomed out my new lock! I ran outside, expecting to see another giant crater in the lawn, but to my relief there wasn't one. I didn't think Ivan could take another digging incident. Then I noticed a scattering of little yellow flowers on the lawn and felt sick. I looked over at Nala's resting place and almost collapsed. The dogs had pulled her mimosa tree over, dug the tree out of the pot, including the roots, snapped off the branches and spread the entire contents of the dirt containing Nala's ashes across the lawn.

I lost it. I ran over to the tree and grabbed a ripped-off branch, waving it wildly whilst screaming at the dogs. Otis jumped up, grabbed the branch and ran off with it, thinking it was a game of chase. I picked up as much of the remains of the tree as I could manage and stomped down to the end of the garden, slipped in dog shit and threw the unsalvageable tree onto the compost heap. I felt like throwing myself onto the heap I was so upset. I scooped up the dirt and Nala's ashes, tears streaming down my face. This was a new low, even for them. Ella had a friend over who was about to be collected by her dad and I couldn't let him see me as this distraught woman on the edge of a breakdown.

I held myself together just long enough to say goodbye and then dropped onto the sofa in floods of tears. Just when I thought things couldn't get any worse, they always managed to sink even lower. It was all too much.

Sunday 24 March

I could barely look at the dogs this morning, I was so upset. I have to remind myself they are not deliberately trying to ruin my life – they are animals, not people. Otis could sense my upset and behaved impeccably all day. He didn't leave my side, following me everywhere. I felt so low. It seemed like every step forward resulted in ten steps backwards and it was so demoralising. The harder I tried the worse things got. I was putting so much time into the dogs and following all the expert's advice but nothing was working. Bringing up a child was a piece of cake compared to this. When I had Ella, I listened to advice, read the relevant books and used my instincts and common sense and had it sussed. Being calm, kind, consistent and confident was the secret to my success. Understanding what her needs were and making sure these were all met, meant she was happy, bright and thriving. It felt completely natural and I loved every second of raising her as a baby, toddler and now little girl. But this was unknown territory and following this blueprint was clearly not effective. It was soul destroying.

I lay on the sofa and put on Friends. Otis's face was inches from mine, and he gave me a big lick. I couldn't stay mad at him, and as I hugged him, his tail spun around like a windmill. He was so happy we were friends again. Kiara didn't give two hoots. It was like nothing had happened. She continued to grab anything she could get hold of, barked at every sound in the street, chased every squirrel in the garden and was her usual disobedient self. I wasn't mad at her, just exhausted by her antics. I stared out at the garden which looked beyond repair at this point. I looked at the state of the room I'd cleared up moments earlier – ripped cushions, decapitated toys, CD cases emptied and just shook my head. I didn't have the energy for it today. None of us did.

Monday 25 March

Ella came home from school with a cute chipmunk she'd made out of clay in her art class. Her teacher said it was so good she should take it home and paint it and bring it back into school tomorrow. Ella was playing with it on the dining table before she ran off to the loo. When she went back into the room I heard her scream.

'NOOOOOOOOOO! Muuuuuuuummmmmmm-mmyyyyyyyyy! Kiara's eaten my chipmunk!'

I rushed in to hear the crunching of clay as Kiara spat out the broken pieces of the little chipmunk. I picked up the tiny pieces and wrapped them in a tissue. It was irreparable. Ella was sobbing. Kiara rolled onto her back and played dead at which point I think Ella wished she was.

'I don't want to have Kiara anymore,' she said through her tears. I hugged her tight. This was not the life any of us had envisioned.

Tuesday 26 March

I hit snooze four times. I didn't want to get up and face the day. Or rather, the dogs.

I'd barely slept from stressing about them. I dragged myself out of bed and let them into the garden, double locking the door behind them. I ignored the barking at the neighbour's dog and made breakfast. I saw several tea towels splayed across the lawn which I must have missed yesterday in all the upset. I couldn't even be bothered to go and get them. What was the point? The pups charged up to the patio door when they saw me, jumping with excitement. I ignored them and walked away. I couldn't deal with them yet.

I dropped Ella at school and took the dogs to the park. I wanted to walk them early so I could get on with work as I was so behind on everything. For the first time in six months, my heart just wasn't in it. I took Kiara first but just as I unclipped the seatbelt from her harness, she slipped her collar and leapt out of the car. I slammed the door shut, leaving Otis inside, and ran after her, furious. She was tearing off into the distance after a jogger. I ran after her, grabbed her, and the man shrieked at me as he jogged off. I held onto Kiara so tightly my knuckles went white. I was not going to budge until he was out of sight. When he was at a safe distance, he stopped, turned around and yelled, 'Your dog is a fucking nutter and you should be locked up! If I find out where you live…' I was completely stunned. Kiara flipped out. She yanked so hard that I lost my grip on her and she raced towards him at a speed I'd not seen since we were thrown out of puppy training. She jumped up and knocked him backwards. He lost it, and I was terrified. Kiara was so scared she ran back to me and the pair of us haired towards the car like our lives depended on it – because they probably did! I could barely see with all the tears streaming down my face. Kiara flew into the car which was steamed-up from Otis, who was frantic from all the barking and shouting. I locked all the doors, put the key in the ignition and tore out of there. Then I sobbed. Full on, pitiful, loud, snotty sobs. I had to face facts – Kiara was out of control and I couldn't deal with her any longer.

Thursday 28 March

Get two puppies, she said. They'll keep each other company, she said. What she failed to mention was that they would chase every living being out of the park, destroy your home, dig craters in the lawn, rip the heads off your plants, bark at anything that moved, lunge at anyone who came into your place and eat you out of house and home!

Although I realise a lot of this behaviour, difficult though it is, is probably normal for sibling puppies, what isn't normal is Kiara's behaviour. It's extreme. Having Otis as a benchmark, it is easy to spot that Kiara's reactions to things are just not right.

Kiara can't relax when we're out *or* at home, unless I remove all stimuli. This means either putting her in her crate and covering it with a fleece or drawing the curtains if we're in the living room. While Otis snores away in a deep slumber, Kiara is wide-eyed, watching and reacting to everything. If there is shouting on the television, she runs behind the sofa. If a bird flies past the window, she races into the garden. If someone walks along our road, she barks madly at the window. It's like she can't switch off. It's exhausting. She is destructive and impulsive and follows no rules inside or outside of the house. Taking her anywhere is stressful at best, dangerous at worst. I can't control her behaviour and I can't control her environment. Even trespassing in deserted areas at ungodly hours isn't working, and quite frankly, it's too much. I can't cope.

The experts I've spoken to are at a loss about what to do with her. She is ruining my life. She is ruining all our lives, including Otis's who is dragged into her chaos and destruction daily. I can't spend the time I need with him because I am constantly dealing with her. I am at my wit's end and I can't do it anymore. Drastic action needs to be taken and I know what it is that I need to do.

Sunday 31 March

I spent the morning looking at bootcamps for dogs with behavioural issues. They looked like correctional facilities for criminals. I couldn't imagine how severely punishing Kiara for her behaviour could possibly help her. She didn't seem like the sort of dog who could take this type of treatment, so I gave them a call.

It was clear these places got results by scaring the living daylights out of the poor animals. They believed the only way to control a dog was to make them submissive. I didn't like our conversation and I didn't like the methods they used. There was no way Kiara was going to a place like that. I needed someone to understand her, not scare her. These bootcamps wouldn't fix her, they would break her. I looked up centres who might be able to help and I came across the Rhodesian Ridgeback Welfare Trust.

As well as preventing irresponsible breeding programmes, the Trust looks after and rehomes Ridgebacks. I spoke to the lovely man who ran it. As I spilled my guts, crying my eyes out, he listened to every word without judgement.

'You are fighting a losing battle keeping them together,' he said kindly. 'It is a lose-lose situation for them and for you. You need to separate them.'

I looked over at Otis and Kiara squished up asleep on the rug together and couldn't imagine them being split up. Their bond was so strong and they loved each other so much.

The man explained to me that they would keep Kiara in the centre for a few weeks before going into foster care for six months while they assessed her and figured out what was wrong. He hesitated for a moment and asked, 'Afterwards, do you want her back?'

The tears streamed down my face. 'Of course I want her back, she's part of our family. I'm just at a loss at what to do,' I said.

'That's wonderful.' He sounded relieved. 'As you can imagine, they are not the easiest dogs to rehome. I'm afraid you can't visit her while she's here. It will only confuse her. Is that okay?'

It was hard for me to comprehend not seeing her for six months. How was I going to explain it to Otis.

He said he'd send the paperwork through tonight and that I could bring all the forms with me when I drive her up tomorrow. I was going to drive 150 miles with Kiara having no idea that when we got there, she wasn't coming back with me. It made me feel sick.

I sat in the garden alone. I'd explained to Ella and Ivan what I was doing and they both fully understood. They could see I had tried everything and still progress was nil.

Jane came over and joined me for a supportive gin.

'You're doing the right thing,' she said softly.

And I really hoped I was. I put the pups to bed with their nightly routine of a treat, played Classical for Pets on Alexa and they both went straight to sleep. This would be Kiara's last night sleeping next to her brother and the last morning we would wake up with them both for six months. I thought I'd feel relief but I didn't. I felt nothing but pain.

I opened my emails and there in the inbox was the email from the Trust as promised.

'Documents to fill out before Surrender' was the subject, and I could see the little paperclip of attachments on the right. I couldn't open the email. Not tonight. I'll fill them out in the morning. I closed the laptop and went to bed. My heart felt like it was breaking.

CHAPTER 9 – APRIL

HOLIDAY SEASON

Age: 9 months
Weight: Otis 40 kg / Kiara 38 kg

Monday 1 April

I'd cried myself to sleep and woke up feeling sick with grief. I took one look at the pups soundly asleep in their beds, and burst into tears. They gave me their usual exuberant greeting, unaware of what was about to happen. I wandered around the kitchen in a trance getting breakfast ready. Kiara followed me everywhere while Otis was in the garden discovering new smells and eating the bamboo.

I sat down on the sofa and couldn't stop the tears. I'd failed. I'd failed my family, I'd failed myself but most of all, I'd failed Kiara. She joined me on the sofa and put her head on my lap, her satin auburn ears dangling over her sad eyes. Her cold wet nose had a tiny white feather stuck to it. In one lick, she swiped it off and attempted to eat it.

'What are we going to do with you?' I whispered to her. She breathed out a big sigh and the wet feather flew up and landed on my lap. I smiled as I ran my finger along the silky crease down the middle of her head. Her eyes flickered and closed. She was the most relaxed I'd ever seen her. Otis was whining outside to be let back in, but I let Kiara enjoy this quiet moment by herself as the overwhelming love I had for this dog poured out of me. As we both sat there peacefully, Kiara breathing heavily while I stroked her softness, I knew deep in my heart that whatever the future held, I couldn't give this dog up, not even for six months.

I couldn't send Kiara somewhere else because I couldn't handle her. If I couldn't fix her with everything I'd tried, what made me certain that someone else could. What if it made her worse? I knew life was never going to be easy with this pup, but if she couldn't depend on her family then who could she depend on? I couldn't desert her. It wasn't in my nature. For better or for worse she belonged here with us, her family. I realised in that moment that just because you don't always get what you expect in life, doesn't mean you abandon it. You deal with it, and that was what I was going to do. Maybe she wasn't a problem to be "fixed". Maybe I had to understand her instead.

I opened my laptop and sent one line to the lovely man at the Trust.

'Thank you so much for your kindness yesterday but I've changed my mind. Kiara will be staying with us.' Then I deleted his email and all its attachments.

Otis came skidding into the living room with his usual FOMO. Kiara jumped off the sofa and they charged down the garden together, causing their usual mayhem. I watched them and smiled. They belong together. And together they belong with us.

Wednesday 3 April

I made an appointment with a top dog behaviourist called Tom. He was great with dogs – people not so much – but I have to say, the guy really knew his stuff. I needed a PhD in animal psychology to understand most of what he said but the bottom line was, he concluded that Kiara had an "emotional impulsive response" to perceived threats. Meaning, that her bolting, barking and lunging are all just ways to scare off the threat in order to feel safe. Threats being defined as pretty much everything and anything in existence. The plan of action was to build her confidence by slowly introducing her to these perceived threats one at a time, from a far enough distance, and then reward her when she didn't react. Over time, we would move nearer until she eventually became desensitised to these "threats" and no longer thought that she was going to be killed by the neighbour's sausage dog, a random squirrel or our postman (although I think that ship has sailed). The main point to take away from this initial consultation was that Kiara wasn't *intentionally* trying to wreck our lives. I relayed all this back to Ivan, who said, 'So, basically you just paid 350 quid to be told that Kiara can't help being a little shit.'

For the first time, I actually had hope that things could improve and for once I was looking forward to a follow-up session with Tom as opposed to dreading it. And you can't put a price on that.

Thursday 4 April

I'm continually reminding myself that just because I'm trying to understand Kiara's behaviour rather than react to it, does not mean that it's less work. It's actually more work in the short term, if that's even possible.

I took Kiara to the gates of the park today to start the new regime of observing other beings, both human and non-human, from the safety of behind bars, i.e., the park gates. She went berserk as soon as we got there, but I ignored her lunging and barking and waited until she calmed down, then rewarded her with a treat. With her adrenaline through the roof, she was too stressed to actually take the treat so I enthusiastically praised her instead so she got the message. I reminded myself that the aim today was to stay at a safe distance until we could move closer in due time, probably five years judging by her reaction. However, this proved impossible for two reasons. Firstly, there was only one entrance in and out of the park, and secondly, it was on a busy stretch of road. Therefore, people, pets and their kids with their scooters, bikes and skateboards were coming at us from every angle. It was like Waterloo Station. There were those entering the park, those leaving the park, those walking past the park and those already in the park. I had to manoeuvre Kiara every which way to avoid bumping into anyone, which made me look like a complete nutjob. People were holding the gate open for me to enter the park and looked at me like I was mad when I said no thanks and then moved Kiara in a circle back to the same spot outside the park gates.

I called it a day when I could see it was enough for Kiara, and I was getting concerned I was about to be reported for loitering. I thought she did really well, especially considering how busy it was, so we headed home. Kiara was so exhausted that she collapsed on the back seat of the car and didn't bark at anything. Every cloud.

Saturday 6 April

I'm trying not to count down the days until we're going on holiday (six days, including today). Ella had her nails painted and I threw in a pedicure as she was so excited about the new massage chairs they'd just installed. I didn't want a mani-pedi but asked if I could pay to use the massage chair as my body was aching from yesterday's stint at the park, but they laughed, thinking I was joking. Ella wanted animal nail art and when asked what animal she'd like on her fingers, she said cats. When they asked what she'd like on her toes, she said pigs. Strangely, no dogs. I declined having anything done and collapsed onto the big squidgy sofa, relishing in having an hour to do absolutely nothing other than inhaling chemicals. My own snoring woke me up. God, I need this holiday.

Sunday 7 April

Ivan and Ella were up before me and were in the garden playing with the pups. I watched from behind the curtains so the pups couldn't see me or they'd be in like a shot. Kiara was weaving in and out of Ivan's legs and Otis was copying her. Ella had to lift a leg up to let Otis through or he'd get stuck he was so tall. Ella threw a ball and Otis ran to get it until Kiara hurled herself at him, knocking him to the floor. She didn't want the ball, she just didn't want him to have it. All four of them went on the trampoline and Ivan was talking to the pups in a voice I hadn't heard before. It was the sort of voice that said, I think I actually rather like you.

Monday 8 April

It was our second session with the behaviourist today. Tom looked as disappointed to see me as he did the first time but he looked delighted to see Kiara. Unfortunately, the feeling wasn't reciprocated and Kiara tried her hardest to get back into the car when she saw Tom, but he didn't take it personally. The plan today was to de-sensitise Kiara to dogs who were close by. I thought this was pushing it for session two, but Tom was the pro and I knew I was in good hands.

I took Kiara into the paddock while Tom went off to get the training dog. This dog was going to sit behind a chain-link fence at the end of the paddock that Kiara and I were in. Tom instructed me to let Kiara off the lead. I unclicked it and Kiara ran at breakneck speed towards the dog, smashing straight into the fence. Even Tom, with his twenty years of experience, looked shaken. When Kiara figured out that she couldn't get to the dog, she barked manically whilst jumping up at the fence, right in the dog's face. Fortunately, the dog was deaf which was lucky because if he wasn't before, he certainly would have been afterwards.

The dog was taken away and Kiara stopped barking. She looked deranged, she was so stressed out. Tom came into the paddock with a serious look on his face. 'In all my years of training, I have never seen a dog with a prey drive as strong as that,' he said. 'The speed at which she reached the dog was staggering. If that fence hadn't been there, she would have broken the dog's legs.' Legs? I was thinking more like his neck, but said nothing.

'You will NEVER be able to let that dog off lead,' he said firmly.

I thought at this point we were going to be thrown out, but instead, he said that he wanted to see whether Kiara's reaction was fear-based or aggression-based. I panicked for a second, thinking that he couldn't possibly think it was a good idea to bring that dog INTO the paddock after what he'd just seen. I looked down at Kiara who was frothing at the mouth from all the adrenalin. Tom said he was going to bring an identical, life-sized stuffed toy into the paddock and see what Kiara did. I stifled a laugh. 'Kiara is never going to believe it's real,' I said.

'In twenty years I have never met a dog who has not been fooled.' And he was right. The second Kiara saw it, she went nuts. She ran towards it, barked furiously, then ran around it in circles until I was dizzy watching. By this point, the entire staff who worked there had come out to see what all the noise was about. It looked like a comedy act. I was flabbergasted that she didn't realise it was a toy. It even fell over at one point and I burst out laughing, but still she barked and ran around it thinking it was real. However, she did not touch it once.

'Well, the good news is that it isn't aggression-based behaviour as she didn't attack the dog. That's not to say she wouldn't attack it if the dog went for her,' Tom said. This was tricky to establish, given that the dog was a stuffed toy. I was interested to know what aggressive behaviour looked like as it didn't look like much fun from where I was standing, so Tom filled me in.

'Last week we had a Boxer dog who knocked me over, jumped on top of the toy dog, ripped off the head, unstuffed it, pissed on it, then left.'

Kiara is a pussy cat compared to that.

Tuesday 9 April
4 days to go 'til our Holiday (and counting)

Kiara is acting strangely today, and by that, I mean more strangely than usual. There's also an odd smell emanating from her. On inspection, I can see she's not rolled in anything suspect but there are a few spots of blood on the floor. I check her pads for cuts but nothing. Otis is sniffing her bum so I look at her private parts and they're swollen. Please God do not let this be my worst nightmare – that Kiara has come into season right before our holiday! A frantic search on Google, along with the spots of blood in her bed, confirm my worst fear. She is in season and it will last three weeks! And it gets worse… she will be most fertile while we are away on holiday. Oh FFS! This could not have come at a worse time.

I call the vets and try calmly to relay my predicament. Once again, my fears are confirmed. 'They have to be separated immediately or they will mate,' Penny tells me. 'You need to put Otis in kennels today.' Putting Otis in kennels for three weeks doesn't bear thinking about.

'I have known dogs chew their way through crates and eat through concrete walls to get to their mate,' she says.

I can't cancel the holiday! Instead, I vow to keep an eye on them 24/7 before we go, and whilst we are away, they will stay in separate rooms. I phone the dog hotel and tell them what's happened. After they commiserate with my bad luck, they tell me they have one space left in kennels and one VIP room left. Obviously two VIP rooms would bankrupt us. They assure me that the kennel they have available is the large one at the end of a row where Otis would have a view of the garden and get to play in it every day. I ask if I can come and take a look right away.

As I walk down a row of what looks like prison cells with either stressed-out or manically depressed canine in-mates, I reach his garden-view accommodation. It is a concrete square no bigger than two metres wide with a tiny opening at the back where he can go and do his "business" on a slab of concrete before returning to his cell, where he'll presumably die from depression or boredom. Either way, he'll never forgive me for doing this to him and he'll certainly never trust me again. My emotions get the better of me and I burst into tears. I tell them that I'd rather not go on holiday than leave him here. He'll absolutely hate it. I'm aware I'm insulting their facilities but I can't help it, and thankfully, they are very understanding. One of the staff members confesses they'd never leave their dog here either and points to a depressed little soul further down the row who has been here for three months while his owners go on their yearly cruise. I can't hide my disgust, particularly when they clearly have the money to pay for a VIP room. Some people don't deserve dogs.

'I'll take the other VIP room, please,' I splutter, my heart palpitating.

I mentally calculate the cost of the two rooms which almost equals the cost of our all-inclusive trip to the Caribbean, but feel that I have no choice. I also feel like I have no sane way of telling Ivan the news so I do what any woman would do in my position and don't tell him. And while I've spent our entire savings on dog accommodation, I throw in a couple of daily walks for them so they can be together, on lead (obviously). In for a penny, in for a pound. Albeit thousands.

Wednesday 10 April

I dropped Ella off at a graffiti art class with her friend while I spent most of the day running after Kiara, blotting her privates so as not to drip blood all over the house, including the cream rug. When I bought the rug, I didn't envision living with two wild ponies in the house with one of them in season. Despite my best efforts, I have blood-stained socks and slippers as well as a blood-stained cream rug. I've been recommended dog nappies but know there's zero chance of those being effective. If Kiara doesn't rip them off and eat them, Otis most certainly will. And I can't help thinking how unnatural and ludicrous they look – I can't put an African lion dog in a nappy. At least I'll get a week off while we're away.

Remarkably, Otis isn't trying to make babies with Kiara but I am keeping a hawk's eye on them just in case, and whenever he sniffs her bum I tell him firmly, NO. Luckily, he seems more curious than horny but it's early days.

Kiara is like a different dog. She's so quiet and just wants to keep to herself. She doesn't join us when we're playing in the garden and she's not interested in going for a walk either, which is actually a blessing as I'm knackered from playing constantly with Otis to distract him. A male dog can smell a bitch in heat from seven miles away so I check the driveway for a queue of horny suitors. So far, so good.

I call Tom for our weekly update and inform him of the latest debacle. He seconds what Penny said, and tells me that if Otis does mount Kiara, I must not try to get him off her as they will be "locked" together, and any attempt to separate them could break his penis! Jesus! I'm tempted to look this up but can't face the thought of what images I might see if I Google "broken dog's penis". Instead, I take his expert word for it. Being on anti-copulation duty means I'm getting naff all else done, like work or packing for the holiday.

Friday 12 April

With only 1 day to go until we leave for Jamaica, I have such a ridiculous number of things to do I need to make a list:

- Buy dog food for the week (20 kilos)
- Collect worming, flea and tick meds from vets (avoid Penny)
- Get dog chews for the week (40 should do)
- Remove squeakers from toys (before Otis does)
- Wash dogs and bedding (and Kiara's stinky reindeer)
- Pack extra dog bedding for Kiara (and bag for blood-stained blankets)
- Wash, dry and iron holiday clothes (okay, forget ironing)
- Collect Ella's allergy meds

- Check Ivan has packed more than one pair of pants
- Pack an army's worth of kids first-aid supplies for every eventuality
- Notify alarm company that guard dogs are away
- Find passports
- Book taxi
- Wax legs
- Paint nails
- Oh, and PACK

Midnight – everything complete but will be going away with hairy legs, smudged nails and no bikinis as Kiara ran off with them somewhere.

I put the pups to bed and have mixed emotions of sadness then euphoria… WE'RE GOING ON HOLIDAY. WOO HOO!

Saturday 13 April

The pups can sense something is up. I don't think they've ever seen me so happy. We load their mountain of things into Ivan's car and the pups and Ella cram into mine. I haven't walked them this morning so there is a lot of pent-up energy. They don't settle on the journey and are a mixture of excitement and confusion. When we reach the dog hotel, they settle down immediately, playing dead. Bigfoot is dozing with one eye open.

We walk them to their VIP rooms which are at the far end of the grounds, passing dozens of frantic dogs. By the time we reach their rooms, they are completely stressed out. Although their rooms are next to each other, they have never been separated before. They've been with each other every day since the day they were born. Ivan leads Kiara into her room and Otis automatically follows. My stomach lurches as I tug him the other way, saying, 'This way,' in an over-jolly manner. I swallow the lump in my throat. Otis pulls so hard to get to Kiara that I have to use my entire body strength to pull him away. It is heart-wrenching. In his room, I lay out all his toys and Ivan sets up his crate, tying the door open and putting fleeces over the sides, like his den at home. I put a large chew on the floor but he's not interested. He scrambles for me to pick him up but I stroke him, give him a kiss and leave. We act confidently to assure him that everything's okay and leave before he sees that we're upset. We do the same with Kiara. She goes straight into her crate and chews her toys.

As we leave, Otis pounds at the door, barking. Kiara doesn't make a sound. I don't know which is worse. Ella is crying and I'm on the brink, but I have to stay strong. I comfort Ella, reminding her that it is only one week, they are right next door to each other and will be walked together twice a day. They have a huge room, their own garden and will be looked after by everyone here. Even though I've never needed a holiday as much as I do now, I felt like cancelling it there and then, but I thought Ivan would divorce me if I did. Or worse, he'd go without me.

At the airport…

The worry and guilt of leaving the pups, coupled with my fear of flying, meant the only way I could get on the plane was with an extra large glass of wine inside me. 11 a.m. is a little early for wine, even for a Brit, but the airport is a different world. It has no time zone so the usual rules don't apply, besides, there were plenty of lads already on their third of fourth beer. As I'd only eaten a bag of crisps since dropping the pups off, I sank into a relaxed state extremely quickly. In my previous life, i.e., pre-dogs, I found travel an annoying necessity to get to my destination, but now the thought of sitting down for ten hours without having to worry about what is being eaten or destroyed is a luxury I can't put a price on (okay, it's a lot). Ten whole hours of doing absolutely nothing is a holiday in itself! I don't care at this point if we don't even land and just spend the time flying around, so long as I can read a book without it being chewed, sip a drink without it being knocked out of my hand, and eat dinner without two puppies drooling at my feet. When the steward jolts me out of my daydream and asks if there's anything he can get me, I want to grab hold of him and kiss him. Instead, I order a G&T and make a promise to myself that I am going to enjoy every single second of this trip, starting from now. I turn off my phone and hold the picture of Otis and Kiara in my mind as I tell them telepathically, I love you both, and I'll be home soon. Please. Be. Good.

Sunday 14 April – Jamaican Bliss!

The hotel is a tropical paradise. The staff are ridiculously attentive and so friendly, the food is mouth-wateringly delicious and the weather absolutely perfect. I sit on the balcony overlooking the beach and check my phone for messages about the dogs. There is one. My heart jumps. Thankfully, it's an email letting me know the dogs have settled in well, eaten their dinner and been for a walk together. Not wanting to sound like a needy pet parent, I reply, asking if they wouldn't mind sending me a couple of photos. They send them right away and the pups look really happy. I sit back and relax on the enormous day bed on our balcony, watching a very happy Ivan and Ella splashing around in the pool. Everyone is happy.

Saturday 20 April

The final day of what has been the most heavenly seven days, ending in a hilarious foam party. I return to the room to check my phone and see three missed calls from the dog hotel and a voicemail. As panic rises, I listen to the message asking for permission to take Kiara to the vets. I fear the worst and call straight back, grateful that the time difference means it's still a working day in England. The lovely receptionist's soft voice calms me and tells me that it's nothing serious. Kiara had her own private foam party in the night by unstuffing the entire sofa in her room. She had an allergic reaction to the stuffing and her tummy is now covered in a red rash. The receptionist sent me a picture and it was similar to the one she'd had from my birthday beanbag (which I deduced from the fact her rash disappeared once the beanbag was annihilated). I said not to take her to the vets (the stress alone would make it worse), and that I'd sort it out when we got back. Now there was just the issue of replacing the sofa. I offered to pay for it but they kindly declined, saying it had been donated. I guessed Kiara had reached her limit with us being away and being separated from her brother, and that it was just an act of acute anxiety. I was so relieved that we were going home tomorrow. I couldn't be happy knowing they were not.

Sunday 21 April

After a long and turbulent flight, we landed, jetlagged and sleep-deprived, but desperate to drive and collect the pups. We had all missed them more that we thought. When we arrived, we were told that there had been two more incidents in the night. After replacing Kiara's sofa with another one, it had met the same fate. Incredulously, when they went into Otis's room, he had also done the exact same thing! I found this remarkable, considering he had no idea what Kiara had done. Could they communicate telepathically or was seven days their threshold of being by themselves? Thank goodness we were home. I offered to pay for all three sofas, tightly crossing my fingers under the counter, but they graciously told me that they were expecting another batch to be delivered later today.

We rushed to see the pups. Ivan and Ella went to Otis's room first and I went to Kiara's. When I opened the door, she was curled up in the far corner of the room. She hadn't seen it was me and rolled onto her back in a submissive position. She looked so scared it was heartbreaking. I called her name and she realised it was me. She scrambled to her feet like Scooby Doo and couldn't get to me fast enough. She jumped into my arms and I hugged her as she licked my face wet. It was so good to see her. When Otis came into the room, he couldn't quite believe it was me. He whimpered and moaned. They were both so out of sorts, heavily panting and slithering between each other. I had never seen this behaviour before and it killed me.

They stood up the whole way home, panting and looking out of the window. Kiara didn't bark once. At home, they were subdued and didn't leave my side. Their tails were down and their eyes were black. I got them straight into their routine to give them some comfort and security, but I was petrified that they were traumatised and scarred for life. I couldn't believe it but I missed their crazy selves. I vowed never to send them away again.

Monday 22 April

Because of the jet lag, Ella woke early and let the dogs out. She came running in to me, elated. 'They are back to normal,' she said, grinning like a Cheshire cat.

Both Otis and Kiara were full of beans, had the sparkle back in their eyes and were wagging their tails so fast, I thought they might take off. What a relief!

As I got out of the shower, Otis nicked the sponge and ran off with it into the garden. Kiara was busy lapping up a carton of oat milk from the floor and the dirty washing from the suitcase was distributed far and wide. I wasn't cross in the slightest. I was just happy that my babies were back and fully functioning as their usual dysfunctional selves.

Tuesday 23 April

Although we weren't out of the danger zone yet – Kiara being in season for another ten days – we thought as a treat and as they've been separated for the past week, we would take the pups for a walk together in the woods. Ella held Kiara and I had Otis. As I opened the front door, Kiara spotted a dog across the street. She yanked herself free of Ella's grip and ran straight into the road at the exact moment a car came speeding past. We heard a scream and I thought that was it, she'd been hit. A gruesome image of Kiara lying in the road, covered in blood, flashed into my mind, when suddenly she raced back across the road where a second car coming from the other direction sped past, missing her by a whisper. It all happened in a matter of seconds. I grabbed her, completely stunned, and still holding my breath. The man across the road was standing with his mouth open in shock. I shut Kiara indoors and went over to him to apologise, still shaken. He was so sweet and understanding. He'd thought Kiara was a goner and couldn't believe she'd just dodged death, twice. Twice? I thought. She's dodged death at least twenty times this month alone. I stroked his little fluff ball of a dog and he jumped up in excitement. He was so light in comparison to my two that his legs felt like two little puffs of cotton wool against me. He was licking my hand as I stroked his soft fuzzy head and I thought to myself, why the hell didn't I get a Cockapoo?

Wednesday 24 April

Despite Kiara now being on lead, she clearly still had a death wish which meant it was time to buy a lead from which she couldn't break free. A Halti lead is a special lead which prevents a dog from pulling. Apparently, if they pull forward, the strap over the nose becomes uncomfortable and so they stop. Whether it would work on Kiara was another matter, but I was willing to give anything a go. I watched a video on how to introduce her to this new style of lead.

1. lay the lead on the floor and give treats every time they sniff it
2. fill hand with treats and lay lead across hand so dog eats treats through the lead
3. put lead on dog for thirty seconds then give treats and take if off
4. put lead on dog for forty seconds then give treats and take it off
5. continue in increments of ten seconds until wearing it for a few minutes

6. do this several times a day then walk dog around garden until they are used to it
7. take dog for a short walk, building up over time until they are used to the lead

Kiara was gagging for a walk and since I'd done everything by the book up to this point, and it had made bugger all difference, I decided to jump straight to stage 7, put the lead on, ply her with masses of treats and go straight out for a walk.

The lead is NOTHING SHORT OF MIRACULOUS. She didn't pull once. She did drag her head along every bush and hedgerow to try and get the thing off, but once she realised it was staying put, she gave up and walked normally. I can't believe that I actually walked my dog along the street looking like a normal human being walking a normal dog. I'm still in shock.

Thursday 25 April

Ivan walked Kiara wearing the Halti lead for the first time. When he returned, he had an expression on his face I couldn't quite decipher which made me think something awful had happened. As I braced myself for the tale of woe, he said, 'I can't believe I'd ever say this about this dog, but she walked to heel the whole way around the block! She was actually chilled.'

I couldn't help but beam with pride. My little girl is making progress at long last. Things are finally looking up.

Friday 26 April

We're all being vigilant watching the pups to make sure they don't mate while Kiara is still on heat. Ivan says, when

I'm not around, the first thing Otis does is make a bee-line for her. When I'm in the same room with them, he stays well away. I wonder if this means he respects me as pack leader, finally. Just to be sure, I put them away separately when I go out, so nothing untoward happens.

I inspected Kiara's rash and it's spread to her armpits. I also noticed something else – her nipples are swollen. It's probably due to the fact that she's still in season and it's possibly not helped by the rash. But there is a niggling feeling eating away at me – please do not let it be that Otis got her pregnant while we were away. Apart from the fact that we've just spent a small fortune to keep them separate by paying for two VIP rooms, the thought of this situation just doesn't bear thinking about.

I call the vets to make an appointment to see Penny first thing on Monday.

Monday 29 April

I arrived early at the vets and left Kiara in the car until Penny was ready so that I didn't stress Kiara out unnecessarily. I got chatting to a young guy who was waiting outside with his little cross-breed and noticed him holding a muzzle. We got chatting and he explained that his dog hates other dogs and wants to kill them on sight, which is why he has to wait outside. The muzzle is to stop him biting Penny. I wanted to do a happy dance to celebrate the fact that I'm not the only person with a crazy canine but instead I chose to make him feel better by regaling some of my own horror stories. This cheered him up no end. My good deed for the day, done.

Poor Kiara needed an anti-inflammatory injection and steroids for her rash! She is not happy with me and neither is my credit card.

I ask Penny about Kiara's swollen nipples and she checks Kiara's tummy.

There is a long pause.

'Her tummy is swollen too,' she says, looking at me. I can't quite process what I'm hearing.

'Is she pregnant?' I ask, panicking.

'It could be a phantom pregnancy but I'm not sure,' she says. 'You'll need to get her scanned.'

The room spins and I feel like I'm about to pass out.

'Letting her have a litter could kill her at this age, plus the puppies being inbred would have severe problems,' she added. Problems? Like I was ever in a million years going to let Kiara have a litter with her genes. The world wasn't big enough to cope with more than one Kiara, let alone an entire litter of them.

She gave me the number of a lady who does house visits with a mobile scanning device and told me to give her a call ASAP.

'If you leave it too late, I won't do an abortion, for ethical reasons,' she says.

I call the scanning lady the moment I'm home and leave her an urgent message. Penny's words haunt me as I try to establish when this could have possibly happened. I call the dog hotel and they confirm the dogs were apart the entire time, except when they were walked together on lead and that was always with two members of staff.

Every scenario makes me feel sick to the stomach. Kiara having an abortion, Kiara dying giving birth, Kiara having thirteen puppies… I pray and I pray that it's just a phantom pregnancy. I can't bear to even think of the alternative.

CHAPTER 10 – MAY

PREGNANCY SCARE

Wednesday 1 May

It was a suffocatingly hot night and I couldn't sleep a wink. This heatwave is never ending! I checked my messages to see whether Lydia, the scanning lady, had called me back. Nothing. It was only 6.00 a.m. so probably a bit early to chase.

I check on Kiara who is uncharacteristically quiet. I remember my cat, Sunny, behaving in a similar way when she was pregnant. The hormones completely softened her. She was a feisty little madam but became so placid when she was pregnant, I barely recognised her. Sunny got knocked up during the winter which was highly unusual, and gave birth to just one little kitten who we named Toby. She was so nurturing towards him. Maybe this would soften Kiara? We kept Toby, thinking Sunny would be heartbroken to lose him, but once he got bigger, she'd had enough of him and used to whack him around the face whenever he went near her. Oh God, what if Kiara is pregnant! I check my phone again and fight the urge to message Lydia. I'll hold off 'til 9.00 a.m.

At 8.59 the phone rang. It was Lydia. I was so pleased to hear from her I started crying (I seem to be crying a lot these days). The good news is she can come and scan Kiara, despite us being out of her area. The bad news is a pregnancy won't show up on the scan for at least another three weeks which might be too late for Penny to perform an abortion. We book the scan for 29th May. Only twenty-eight more sleepless nights to go.

Thursday 2 May

Kiara's tummy is definitely getting bigger, and it's not my imagination. I momentarily fantasise of a houseful of Ridgeback puppies and remember fondly how gorgeous Jasmine's litter were. Then I snap back to reality and realise what a nightmare scenario it would actually be. Not to mention the fact that Kiara might die. Rather than spend the next twenty-eight days tormenting myself with worst case scenarios, I decide to be positive and trust that God would not be this cruel, and that it must be a phantom pregnancy and try to get on with life as usual. With Kiara's new mellowness, now might be a good opportunity to introduce some more training as she has lost the urge to chase after anything that moves. Silver linings. I'd researched a trainer who specialises in reactive dogs – the Dog Guardian – and watched countless videos on his successful techniques. I called him and booked a day's session for next week with Otis and his pregnant sister.

Saturday 4 May

We're having a dinner party with ten friends tonight. It's a fully-catered Thai dinner party which we won in a charity auction at school. I could do with something to take my mind off of this shit-show. We've moved the dining table into the kitchen as it's cooler, and put the dog's beds in the living room as I imagine Kiara, in her current state, would want to be as far away from the noise as possible. I am not going to mention to anyone that she might be pregnant – we are already the talk of the school.

Our guests are barely over the threshold before Ivan tells them Kiara is pregnant. Trying not to look annoyed I correct him, explaining that it's a phantom pregnancy and I brush the whole thing off. I give him a look to shut him up which he doesn't understand and just says, 'What?' genuinely perplexed. Men! Despite the evening becoming rowdier the more wine is consumed, Kiara spends the entire night in the kitchen with us where I can see her protruding belly from my seat. Midway through the night, Otis rolls in fox poo in the garden and makes the whole house reek. I have no choice but to shower him and light all my expensive scented candles just to mask the smell. It takes three showers to get the stench off him! I have half a mind to throw him in the bath with one of Ella's Lush bath bombs – those things could mask the smell of a sewage explosion, they're so strong. Well, it did keep my mind off things, I suppose.

Sunday 5 May

Otis is really getting on Kiara's nerves now she's so hormonal, so we allow her to go upstairs and hang out in Ivan's den. Ivan is okay with this now that she's no longer dripping blood or rolling in fox poo. Otis is not okay with this as he's not allowed upstairs, and he's very vocal about it. He keeps putting his front paws on the bottom stair and when I tell him, no, he cries and whines like a big baby. When I go upstairs to check on Kiara, he yowls as if he's missing out on the time of his life. His FOMO is killing him, poor pup. It's not helping that Kiara keeps winding him up by standing at the top of the stairs, sticking her bum in the air then flouncing off into Ivan's den. However, Otis is being such a good boy and not budging, despite every fibre of his being wanting to charge up those stairs like his life depends on it. I reward him with a large chew for his good behaviour but he's not interested. He's only happy when Kiara comes back downstairs. She has taken to coming downstairs frequently just to show Otis that she can go straight back up again – and he can't. She is such a wind-up merchant.

Monday 6 May

Otis is confused as to why Kiara currently hates him. When he approaches her, she growls at him – although it's a bit late for that! She walks past him without even acknowledging his existence, despite his best efforts to entice play. Jumping around and bringing all her favourite squeaky toys are met with complete and utter disdain. She actually sticks her nose in the air like a snooty madam. When he hears a noise outside which usually triggers her, he jumps up and wags his tail in anticipation for her reaction, but she just raises her head, takes a nonchalant look out of the window, and rests it down again. I feel so sorry for him. He must think she's been replaced with an imposter.

Ella and I take Otis to my folk's house to give him some extra attention. Unfortunately, this does not go well. Barney, their cat, is in the kitchen, and when Otis spots him, he makes a dive for him. Barney jumps two metres in the air and leaps on top of the boiler which only has two inches of headroom. He stays up there, wide-eyed and petrified, the entire time we're there. Otis has never seen a cat before and it did not look like he was planning on being friends with him. Luckily, Otis was on lead or I dread to think what might have happened. I hope Barney's okay.

Tuesday 7 May

Mum called to tell me that Otis is banned from their house as she's worried about the cat. Apparently, he didn't come down from the boiler all night as he was so traumatised.

He spent all day hiding in a cupboard in fear of a giant cat-eating monster. I was about to suggest that we come over again to get him used to Otis, but worried I might end up being banned too.

Thursday 9 May – The Dog Guardian

The Dog Guardian is coming to coach us on how to deal with sibling behavioural issues (of which there are more than I can count). With absolutely no books on this subject matter whatsoever (presumably because nobody is stupid enough to get siblings), I was bordering on hyperventilating, I was so excited. When he called to say that he had a terrible cold and would I mind him coming over while he was highly contagious, I replied rather too quickly, 'No, not at all. Come over!' I realise the usual response would be to postpone the session for the sake of his health and ours, but when you're desperate all logic and common sense go out of the window. I did add, 'Only if you're up to it,' so as not to sound like a completely heartless bitch. Luckily, he was willing to take the three-hour train journey despite his nasty cold.

As he walked through the door, I confess, he looked terrible. And I felt guilty for dragging him out when he clearly felt like death warmed up.

I'd shut the dogs behind the baby gate and they were barking loudly at him, but Nigel was as cool as a cucumber. The usual panic I get when someone the dogs don't know comes into the house, melted away. Here was a man whose job it was to help people in need with dogs who were basically out of control. I'd forgotten what it was like to actually relax knowing that someone else – someone with way more knowledge, experience, and hopefully, success – was here to solve my problems. Hallelujah!

Nigel walked into the kitchen where the dogs were, without a care in the world. He didn't bat an eyelid when Kiara barked at him. He talked to me and Ivan without even acknowledging the dogs and told us to do the same. Every time one of them jumped up, he turned his back on them and continued to talk to us in his calm and gentle manner.

As we made our way into the living room, Kiara was distracted by a noise outside and bombed it into the garden, barking and pounding at the neighbour's fence. Otis joined in. For once, I was actually pleased so he could witness their behaviour, but Nigel didn't look in the least bit perturbed.

'Let's go outside,' he said, watching as they continued barking at the neighbours who were in their garden chatting. He pushed his way in front of both dogs, splayed himself across the fence like a splattered starfish and simply said the word "safe" firmly to the dogs. Next, he made exaggerated movements by looking around as if there was an intruder and once again said, 'Safe.' Ivan and I looked at each other, and the dogs looked at each other, bemused. Nigel went back indoors and told us to follow.

He explained that the dogs are taking control of all dangers in or near their territory because *we* are not. First, we have to get things under control at home before we can expect any behavioural changes when we go out. Which means we have to *physically* show them that we are in charge so they don't feel they need to be. Each day must start with me patrolling the perimeter of the garden with them locked indoors watching me. This shows them that I am taking care of things. Whenever they bark at the fence or window, I have to push in front of them, splay myself across the fence or window, and look around with exaggerated movements, then say the word "safe".

They have three chances to correct their behaviour after which time, I have to shut them in the bathroom for time-out to show them there are consequences. However, the bathroom is one of their favourite places, with all its potential hazards, so this would be more of a reward than a consequence. They're too big to fit in the laundry room, and I'm certainly not locking the pair of them in our bedrooms or they'll be un-fit for purpose by bedtime. Instead, I optimistically hope that being an intelligent breed, they'll cotton on and won't need any time-out location to think about their actions.

It was an exhausting but enlightening day and I was determined to put all Nigel's techniques into action. Tomorrow. Today I needed to relax and absorb all this information which meant pulling all the curtains closed, even though it was broad daylight, and keeping the pups in the living room with me so I could keep an eye on them. I filed away all the notes and diagrams Nigel had left for me before the shredding machine – aka Kiara – got hold of them.

Friday 10 May

I follow all Nigel's techniques to the letter and am absolutely shattered by 10.30 a.m. I hadn't realised how many times Kiara barks at the window. It's every ten minutes! I've got half a mind to black out all the windows but I know this wouldn't help solve the problem, plus living in darkness isn't the best idea in summer. Also, the neighbours will think I'm growing marijuana, which would be understandable given the circumstances.

Literally everything triggers Kiara – dogs, people, cars, motorbikes, foxes, birds, squirrels, twigs, leaves, insects, microorganisms. Half the time I can't even see what she's barking at and I'm splayed across the window like I'm being held hostage and hoping someone will see me and rescue me (which is partly true). I need to email Nigel to ask how long until these methods will start showing results. I know that three hours is expecting miracles, but the thought of doing this for weeks on end is going to be logistically impossible. Unless Ivan and Ella check into a hotel while I take time off to spend my days splattered across fence panels and windows, it's not going to work. I don't even want to imagine what passers-by must think.

Saturday 11 May

Ella has agreed that to earn her pocket money this week, she can take over "safe duty", as I'm now calling it. At nine years old, this is highly preferable to washing my car, so I enjoy a lovely morning cuppa whilst watching Saturday Kitchen Live. The pups are outside with Ella who is plastered against various fence panels around the garden. She is incredibly good at it and fortunately the dogs are very receptive to her.

Unsurprisingly, I spend the evening removing tiny splinters from Ella's fingertips but the upside is, she wants to do it again next Saturday. I'll give her an extra monetary bonus along with her pocket money to keep her sweet.

Monday 13 May

Awful news tonight. Our lovely neighbours (the ones who like us), have lost their little dog, Pip. He went missing in the early evening. We were all out looking for him when we heard a bloodcurdling scream from their garden. Their daughter had found him in their swimming pool. He was blind, and had run outside upon hearing a fox and had fallen into the pool and drowned. Our neighbour was beside herself with grief. It was heartbreaking.

'Look after those puppies of yours. No matter what a pain they are, just cherish them,' she said.

I gave both pups a big cuddle and told them how much I loved them. The thought of anything happening to them was unbearable. RIP little Pip.

Tuesday 14 May

With Ella's music exams looming, I have promised to put the whole evening aside to help her practise. I give her my full attention whilst surreptitiously removing Hatchimal Pixies from Otis's mouth. I spot the M&S shopping bag in the garden, and Kiara munching her way through two sundried tomato tartlets which I'd bought for Ivan. The expression, *your dinner is in the dog*, is very apt in this house! However, my attention to Ella doesn't falter and she makes brilliant progress. I am becoming an authority on multi-tasking. Or I've given up caring, I'm not sure which.

Wednesday 15 May

I drop Ella off early for music practice and assure her that I'll be at her assembly on time. She has a solo and I can't miss it. When I get home, Otis shoots out of his crate but Kiara doesn't move. Trying not to freak out about the potential pregnancy disaster, I give her a stroke and see milk leaking from one of her nipples. Stricken with panic, I gently touch it to make sure and it is most definitely milk. My mind races to the worst-case scenario of Kiara dying during birth and us being left with half-a-dozen inbred puppies whilst the unborn others die along with her. Then I imagine the alternative – the horror of aborting a dozen innocent puppies – and I want to throw up. Even if I could find another vet to do the abortion, it would be barbaric. It's more than my mind can cope with today. I cuddle Kiara and tell her everything will be alright. I look up "leaking milk during a phantom pregnancy" and although rare, it does happen. I console myself that everything about this pup is rare but I have this awful sinking feeling in the pit of my stomach that won't go away.

Thursday 16 May

Nigel's techniques have been going pretty well, apart from me looking and feeling like a total prat. Kiara is so subdued that it hasn't been so much of a problem as she's become more couch potato than Road Runner. It's also made it blatantly clear that she's the initiator of all the trouble as there have been very few incidents since she's been knocked up. Otis is only her backup, albeit an incredibly good one, unfortunately for me. I'm hoping that Kiara is realising how chilled life can be without all her shenanigans, and how happy we all are when she's not up to no good. I guess time will tell, although I'm not holding my breath.

I didn't feel it was fair to take Kiara to the park and do the training methods in her current condition as I didn't want to cause her too much stress. I took her to the cemetery for a quiet walk at lunch time, instead. A young couple were visiting the grave of their beloved nan when Kiara spotted them, and kicked off with her usual barking and lunging. So much for being subdued. I made a swift move to get back to the car and leave the couple in peace, when they approached us. Oh God, I thought, here we go – another bollocking. However, to my surprise, they were really sweet. I apologised for the barking and justified bringing her here as she's a rescue dog, which is now my go-to story when she's kicking off. The young guy asked if it was safe to stroke her and I said it was. As he stroked her, he told me about his own rescue dog and how he behaves exactly the same way.

As relief set in, he asked, 'Where did you rescue her from, which centre?'

Taken aback, I thought quickly.

'A family, actually,' I said. And then the questions came thick and fast. Why was she rescued? How long have you had her? Who were the owners? Etc. Gulp!

'She over reacts to any stimulus. The owners couldn't control her. They tried so many methods and it was getting really difficult and expensive. But we are making real progress compared to what she was like when we got her.'

Everything I said was the absolute truth. I just omitted the fact that the "previous" owner was me.

Saturday 18 May

Going to a friend's 40th tonight. Jane is going to pup-sit and Ella has already set up the Dog Bingo game. I can see Ella has pre-chosen her board with the Ridgeback on it and it makes me smile. I watch as Kiara and Ella cuddle up together on the sofa – she really does love this pup. Kiara is nuzzled right into Ella like a ball and Ella is stroking her satin ears inadvertently whilst watching the Cinderella movie. I feel Kiara's tummy for any movement. I know expecting to feel twelve wriggling puppies at this stage is ridiculous, but there is some comfort in feeling no movement. FOMO Otis nudges me so hard for attention, I almost fall off the sofa. He senses that I'm going out and has been sticking to me like a limpet since I put my make-up on (a rare feat these days). They both go nuts when Jane arrives (I see she's wearing her puppy-proof clothing, the ripped coat and dark jeans). She enjoys them jumping up so I allow the rules to be broken for her. They are so happy she is here that they don't mind when we go out. They trot into the living room after her, and I can see they are going to have a fun night in. I'm so drained at the moment, I'd actually rather stay in with them and play dog bingo.

Sunday 19 May

The neighbours with the yappy dog have had a deafeningly loud garden party all day and now it's well into the night and there is no sign of it stopping. Unfortunately, their dog's barking at the fence all bloody day has not been drowned out by their powerful outdoor PA system. Otis and Kiara have been testing my patience by continuously running down there to bark back at the little shit. It's too hot to shut them inside today and I've been down there doing the splaying thing more times than I can count. If I was wearing a pedometer, it would have exploded. I'm hot, sweaty, my legs are killing me and still Otis and Kiara show no sign of stopping. The neighbours know I can't text them to keep it down since I'm indebted to them until I die or we move, whichever comes the soonest. So, I'm going to have to put up with the noise and the pups barking into the early hours of the morning. Great!

Tuesday 21 May

The point of a garden office is to get away from all the distractions in the house and actually get some work done. The pups did not get this memo and are fighting over the top spot in the office. They both want to lie under my desk in the sunny spot but now they are so big, there is only room for one. Otis nabbed it first, but as he stood up to curl into a comfortable sleeping position, Kiara was in there like a shot, leaving him straddled over her. As she shows no sign of moving, he's resigned himself to the wooden chair and somehow manages to contort himself into an awkward sleeping position.

It's crazy that just a few yards away in the house are two huge dog beds and a comfy sofa for four, and yet they'd rather be in here with me, squashed into a chair or lying on a wooden floor. That's what you call love.

As they snore away, I glance around the office at my chewed pen lids, cables with teeth marks and my flask with its dented lid. Even after these pups are no longer around, their marks will be here forever.

Thursday 23 May

Otis snapped at a dog on his walk this morning. He's never done this before and he wasn't provoked (unless the dog sticking his nose up his bum counts). It was only a warning snap, but a dog of his size scares the living daylights out of other dogs, and especially their owners. I see small dogs barking, lunging and snapping at other dogs all the time and it's just brushed off, but when it's a large dog, they are quickly branded a "dangerous dog". Otis is such a gentle giant, I would hate for him to be tarnished in this way, but recently he has been different. He doesn't like any dogs approaching him and short of me shouting out to owners, 'keep your dog away' as they're bounding towards us, I'm not sure what else to do.

I call Tom when I get home and he says it's because Otis is still intact, i.e. got his balls. He explains that Otis's testosterone is surging now that he's ten months old and he won't like other male dogs. More worryingly, they won't like him. I explain that Otis never goes up to other dogs when we're out (successful training tick for me), but he says most owners are idiots (his words) and aren't as responsible as I am (me, responsible? Yay!). He says most owners let their dogs run up to anyone and can't get their dogs back when they call them because they haven't put in the training work.

'It's extremely bad manners to let your dog run up to another dog,' Tom says. 'That dog might have health issues, be old or be a nervous rescue dog.' He was on a roll. 'You should never let your dog approach another dog unless invited.' He was right, as usual. I'd not thought about it like that before. I must pass this information on to Kiara.

Tom suggested keeping Otis on lead and wearing a muzzle until he was castrated. But that was not supposed to be until he was two years old, when his hormones settle, and was another fourteen months away! The last thing I need right now is for more behavioural problems but the thought of him wearing a muzzle seemed excessive.

'Won't a muzzle make him look aggressive?' I asked.

'Exactly. And that will definitely make owners think twice before allowing their dogs to run up to him.' He had a point.

On the drive home, I bought a plastic muzzle which made Otis look like Hannibal Lecter. It was so big, it could carry a basket of eggs.

Friday 24 May

It's the Bank Holiday weekend and the start of half term. We're not going away like we usually do, for obvious reasons. So, instead we have a fun-filled week of activities planned, including the not-so-fun-but-necessary pregnancy scan on Wednesday which is marked in bold on the family calendar.

Half-term plans and dog-sitting requirements:

Saturday – Ella's drama awards ceremony (dog-sitter)
Sunday – Secret Life of Pets 2 movie (Ivan dog-sitting)
Monday – Girls' day – Nails and sushi (dog-sitter)
Tuesday – Ella at Art class with friend
Wednesday – KIARA'S SCAN (buy champagne if not pregnant, gin if she is)
Thursday – Ella at Granny's for the day (me drowning my sorrows or celebrating)
Friday – Ella at sewing class with friends (me possibly still drinking)
Saturday – Ella at audition and Ivan out (dog-sitter)
Sunday – find second job to cover dog-sitting costs. And find dog-sitter.

Saturday 25 May

Amazing day watching Ella's show and picking up her award for Junior Performer of the Year. Fortunately, the cup is made of metal and cannot be chewed or digested by the pups. Therefore, it can actually go on display at home, unlike any of her other awards and prizes.

Sunday 26 May

Ivan agreed to walk Otis while we went to the cinema. Kiara isn't bothered about walks while she's so lethargic. As her penchant for looking for trouble is currently quashed, I don't bother shutting her away and just let her sleep on the sofa.

The movie was hilarious and made me happy that the pups had each other for company. It must be so lonely being left on your own when your owners go out.

When we got home, Ivan was out walking Otis and Kiara was fast asleep on the sofa where we'd left her. She mustered just enough energy to greet us and then went back to her spot. There were neon pompoms all over the hallway from Ella's Greek sandals so she hadn't completely lost her keenness for destruction.

The front door slammed and Ivan came storming in, threw the lead on the floor, charged straight past us without saying a word and stomped upstairs. Otis, head down, went straight into his bed.

Ivan had taken Otis for a walk along the lake and had stopped to sit on a bench and take in the view. He'd tied Otis's lead to the arm of the bench. Whilst admiring the view, he didn't notice a dog coming up from behind but Otis did. Otis took off and chased after the dog, taking the arm of the bench with him. Ivan was leaning on the arm at the time and has bruised all his muscles – along with his ego. Chasing after a dog with a bench arm attached must have been embarrassing to say the least! These two are not doing themselves any favours in winning Ivan over!

Monday 27 May

Ella and I went to TK Maxx to get the pups some new toys. Even though the lifespan of a toy is less that the lifespan of a mayfly (24 hours) they still need stimulation, and I prefer them to chew on dog toys rather than the furniture. The charity shop is currently in short supply of shoes, apparently.

Ella found a neon green bone the size of a small dog which was made of natural rubber (not sure how natural the neon green colouring was), and we bought them some more tennis balls.

The pups took no interest whatsoever in the bone and not much more in the tennis balls but were very curious about what was in our shopping bags, namely Krispy Kremes and Hatchimal replacements. After we ensured these were out of reach, the pups went outside where we'd thrown their new toys. Otis, who now cocks his leg to wee instead of squatting, is taking perfect aim and weeing straight onto the neon bone. Kiara is burying the tennis balls.

Tuesday 28 May

Kiara was up for a walk today which I took as a good sign. I daren't ask Ivan to take her as he's had enough of the "muppets" as he now refers to them. As it was another steaming hot day, I waited until early evening when it was cooler and hopefully quiet. It had been a while since Kiara had last seen a dog and I didn't want any drama.

The pavement was heaving with dog-walkers as though they'd all been released as the clock struck seven!

To avoid confrontation, I spent most of the walk ducking behind parked cars and diving into bushes with Kiara. This worked for the majority of the walk and then I became unstuck. Two Alsatians were heading towards us and a Husky was approaching from behind. With no cars parked on this posh stretch of road I had no choice but to duck into the driveway of a large mansion. Half-a-dozen Mercs and SUVs filled the driveway so I crouched behind one of them with Kiara, and scattered treats on the ground to distract her until all three dogs had passed. I peered from behind the car and could see they were all in front of the house now, but nobody was going anywhere. It was sod's law that the owners knew each other and had stopped for a chat. Kiara was agitated and I was running out of treats, but they carried on their conversation as if they had all the time in the world. My legs were shaking from squatting and now the treats were finished. Kiara was darting around, totally confused as to what the hell we were doing here. An ear-piercing scream from behind made us both jump out of our skin. The owner of the house came out and after spotting a strange woman squatting behind her Merc – presumably a burglar, and holding a large, slightly crackers dog – screamed at the top of her lungs. I leapt up to explain the situation.

'I'm so sorry. It's not what it looks like,' I gabbled. 'I'm hiding in your driveway because my dog is terrified of dogs.'

'I'M TERRIFIED OF DOGS!' she shrieked. Her two daughters came running outside to see what on earth was going on.

'I'm so sorry,' I said. I scarpered out of the driveway and ran home as fast as my legs would carry me. Kiara didn't have any time to react to any passers-by for once as I was behaving more bonkers than her. What that must have looked like on their CCTV footage, I can only imagine.

Wednesday 29 May – The Scan

D-Day is finally here. In a few hours, we will know one way or the other whether Kiara is pregnant.

Lydia turned up right on time, holding a small black case and looking very official. I offered her tea or coffee but she wanted neither. She set up her screen and scanning device without saying a word. Kiara and I watched her and I had to remind myself to breathe.

'If you could bring Kiara over please,' she said, matter-of-factly.

I wasn't sure what to expect but having had several ultrasound scans myself when I was pregnant, I thought there would be a bit more of a ritual involved, especially with such a momentous reveal about to be made. I mean, I wasn't expecting fireworks but Lydia could have been photocopying a document with the lack of song and dance she made about it.

Kiara stood there, calm and collected while this stranger poked around her belly with her device. I held my breath the entire time.

When she had finished scanning Kiara, she put the device down, giving nothing away. Zooming into the screen, she squinted at it carefully. You could hear a pin drop.

'Nothing there,' she said. 'Kiara is not pregnant.' It took a few seconds to register.

'Are you absolutely sure?' I asked.

'One hundred per cent,' she said.

'So, it's a phantom pregnancy?'

'Yes,' she said. 'She'll be back to herself in a few weeks.'

An entire month's worth of anxiety melted away in a heartbeat. I have never been more relieved about anything in my whole life.

Without any fuss, Lydia packed up her equipment and was gone. The whole thing had taken less than ten minutes. I looked at Kiara who was sitting on the floor, confused. She looked up at me with her big doe eyes and I knelt down next to her.

'You are not going to be a mummy, Kiara. Your body just thinks you are. You certainly know how to put us through the wringer, but luckily for you, we love you.' I hugged her and she leaned into me with all her weight for the first time, as tears of relief poured out of me.

CHAPTER 11 – JUNE

KIARA GETS DIAGNOSED

Saturday 1 June

I slept like a log last night for the first time in weeks. Waking up safe in the knowledge that Kiara isn't going to die giving birth to a litter of two-headed puppies feels like I've dodged the biggest bullet in the world. Finally, some good news.

Ella has an audition in Regent's Park. As it's a beautiful day (and not scorching), and I'm on cloud nine, we are going to make a day of it. Ivan has happily agreed to pup-sit given the good news. Although Kiara still looks pregnant, her nipples are no longer swollen so it appears that the phantom pregnancy is finally coming to an end. She has been so withdrawn for the last month I'm actually looking forward to her feeling like her old self again – although I'm hoping her madness will continue to be somewhat subdued, which is possible, given that she's been through such a hormonal milestone. Only time will tell.

Sunday 2 June

I've been teaching Otis how to play "fetch" in the garden and he's doing so well that Ella and I decide to take him to the park to practise.

What I'd failed to teach Otis is that "fetch" only applies when I'm throwing *his* ball and not when other people throw balls for their dogs. Consequently, Otis thinks it's a free-for-all and the first dog to get the ball is the winner.

As a lady threw a ball for her Spaniel, Otis took off, caught the ball and then bombed it around the park with it in his mouth, doing a lap of honour. The Spaniel instinctively chased after Otis, then halfway around had a change of heart, panicked and ran back to his family. Otis mistook this for a game of chase and tore after him to where his family were sitting enjoying tea and cake.

They jumped up in horror as 40 kilos of muscle sped towards them. 'KEEP STILL! DON'T MOVE OR HE'LL BREAK YOUR LEGS!' I yelled. Ignoring my advice, they all dispersed in different directions as Otis ran through their picnic and caught up with the terrified dog. I called for him as the family shouted various accusations at me which, fortunately, I couldn't make out as we were too far away. Otis ran back, dropped the soggy ball at my feet and wagged his tail with glee, completely unaware of the chaos he'd caused.

'You can open your eyes now, Ella,' I said, as I threw the ball back to them and got out of there, making a mental note to add this park to the growing list of places to avoid for the next few weeks.

Tuesday 4 June

As Kiara's recent activity level has been that of a sloth, the length of her claws would give Cruella de Ville a run for her money. Now she's getting her energy back, I thought it best to get them trimmed before she does any damage with these dangerous weapons. As she hates them being trimmed, I thought that rather than traumatise her at home I'd book a dog salon to get them done "professionally". Not only would they be better equipped, but she would bear a grudge against them instead of me. I took Otis along to make her less anxious.

I lead both pups into the gleaming waiting area. They eyed every angle for an escape route but it had glass walls so this was not an option. Even these dogs had not managed to find a way to scale a glass wall. There was a waist-high gate separating the waiting room from the salon which had slats so the dogs could see each other but not get to each other. No sooner was Kiara in the salon, she jumped over the gate and was back in the waiting area with Otis. We dragged Kiara back into the salon area while Otis squashed his nose through one of the slats to check we weren't killing his sister. Kiara thrashed about to get out of my grip but I held her harness tight as the salon owner called for backup. Two assistants appeared from out the back to help us with the procedure. It took four adults to clip the nails of one mad dog. One girl, along with me, held Kiara still, the second girl held Kiara's paw while the third one clipped the nails. Kiara wailed and yelped while Otis pounded the barrier. You'd have thought we were amputating her paws by the fuss she was making. We were attempting the second paw when Kiara shoved the girl, knocking her over, and I lost my grip on her. In one swift move, Kiara leapt over the gate back to Otis, so we called it a day.

In twenty minutes, we'd only managed to cut the nails on one paw. She sounded like she only had three legs when she tip-tapped out of there.

I paid the bill and one of the girls called out, 'We can do the other paws next week.'

If Kiara thought for one second she was coming back to this place, I knew without a doubt, she'd find a way to scale that glass wall.

Wednesday 5 June

I've been surprised by friends with tickets to see Hugh Jackman at the O2 tonight, so I'm taking the pups for a late walk to wear them out so they won't be a pain when Ivan looks after them. They are in serious need of earning some brownie points with him.

I took Otis to the lake and saw that the one-armed bench hadn't been repaired yet. Otis weed against his old ruin then trotted off to smell random dog poos other owners hadn't bothered to pick up. What is it with people thinking it's okay to leave dog poo when they take their dogs out?! It's bad enough when they are left in places where you're allowed to walk dogs, but when you're trespassing on private land, it's inexcusable. I'm picking up other people's dog shit just so they don't think it's Otis's. People must think there is something wrong with my dog's bowels when they see me carrying five bags of poo back to the car. Annoyingly, there are no bins here so I have to travel home in the car with the bags giving off a nuclear stench strong enough to kill a small country.

Thursday 6 June

One month until the pups turn one! When I tell people they're almost a year, they usually say, 'OMG, already? That's gone so quickly!' which makes me want to slap them. You wouldn't say that to someone who's just reached their parole date after a year banged up.

Heading towards this one-year mark, when the pups will no longer be four-legged lunatics but mature adolescents, fills me with optimism. I've been willing my life away for this moment. This moment is catastrophically crushed when I bump into fellow Ridgeback owner at school who drops the bombshell that large breeds stay puppies until they're two years old and don't even begin to calm down until then. Fighting the urge to throw myself onto the playground floor screaming, *why me?* I tell myself that this can't be true – she must have forgotten as it was so long ago. I convince myself of this the whole way home until I am able to Google it and discover that, sure enough, it is true. Then I throw myself onto the rug and cry out in loud sobs, *why me?*

Friday 7 June

Kiara's tummy is shrinking fast so I call Penny to see when I can book her in to be spayed as there is no way I can go through another month like the last. My heart couldn't take it.

'She'll need to go through another season before we spay her,' Penny says.

Crestfallen, I ask what she means.

'As she's a large breed, we need to wait until she's older and has matured a bit,' she says.

'But what if she never matures? Can't we do it now?' I plead.

'If we do it too soon, Kiara could stay in her immature state for the rest of her life.'

Oh God.

'It's not too long. She should have her second season in 6 to 7 months' time,' Penny assures me.

Brilliant, so I either risk her being stuck as a loon for life or according to Penny's timing, have Kiara in season at CHRISTMAS! If I'm being punished from a past life, I must have been a heinous serial killer.

Saturday 8 June

I wake up to some ecstatic news, for me at least! Ella's Godfather has managed to wangle tickets to see Lady Gaga. There is one problem – the concert is in Vegas. And the other slight hitch is, it's next Friday. My bestie is meeting me there from LA and both Gemma and Jane have offered to help Ivan out with the pups. I'm frantically searching for flights to get me out on Thursday and back on Saturday so I'm back in time for Father's Day. I know it's a lot to ask but these are once-in-a-lifetime tickets, and I'm determined to make it work. Knowing what a huge Gaga fan I am, Ivan is supportive and even offers to drop me at the airport. The thought of flying solo makes me hyperventilate so I've booked hypnotherapy sessions for every day before I go so I don't die from a panic attack on the plane. I've almost made it to a year with the pups without dying from stress, I don't want to blow it now.

Sunday 9 June

Otis's testosterone surge is getting worse. Although he's not interested in mounting other dogs – which I count as a blessing – he's instead developed a menacing growl which he demonstrates with great aplomb when we're out on walks. If looks from fellow dog-walkers could kill, I'd be six feet under. I've spoken to Tom about this and he says it's time to use the muzzle. Just as a safety measure.

Reluctantly, I took Otis out wearing the muzzle and he dragged his head along the floor for the entire walk, looking like a demented dog. He only raised his head to growl at any confused dog who trotted over to see what he was doing. People are now giving us a wide berth but it is not because of the muzzle.

Monday 10 June

I've found flights to Vegas for Thursday afternoon, returning Saturday night. A seventy-two-hour round-trip to Vegas makes me feel very rock 'n' roll. A far cry from my current life. There's a lot to pack in before Thursday and I need to get Ivan's Father's Day present pronto before I forget. And it needs to be good, to keep him sweet. Some generous garden vouchers and a pair of heavy-duty gardening gloves should do the trick.

I took Otis for an evening walk by the lake and noticed they'd fixed the bench. I also noticed large signs everywhere saying "It is PROHIBITED to walk dogs in these grounds – which are for MEMBERS ONLY". The huge signs were red and yellow, like a toxic warning, which is a bit over the top if you ask me. I've never even seen anyone in these grounds. Fortunately, Otis can't read so we're still going. Unless I'm asked in person to leave the grounds or escorted off the premises, I think it's worth the risk. It would be a waste not to enjoy the flora and fauna. This might not wash with the management and it will be hard to play dumb if I'm caught out as you'd have to be blind not to see the notices which are every twenty metres or so. Which got me thinking. I wonder how difficult it is to get a white stick. No one would dare approach me if they thought I was blind. Although driving home might be a giveaway.

Tuesday 11 June

Tom told me about a place called the Fields of Freedom where you can hire an entire field for your dogs for an hour. It's fenced off and no other dogs are allowed in during your allotted time. It was specifically created for dogs who didn't like other dogs but who still needed a good run. You can book it for as many days as you like and take as many dogs with you as you want, just as long as you pick up their mess and lock up promptly at the end of your session time. You didn't want to bump into the next customer, given that those dogs also hated dogs! It was absolutely perfect. Cutting down from four walks a day to just one would be life-changing. I couldn't believe it was only twenty minutes from us. How did I not know of this place before! I called the second I got off the phone to Tom and booked a session for the next day, plus an additional two sessions every week for the next month. I was like a kid at Christmas.

Wednesday 12 June

I was super excited to be taking the pups to the Fields of Freedom today. Finally, a chance to run together at full speed without risk of injury or death for any bystanders. The pups sensed my excitement and didn't settle for the entire journey. I couldn't wait for them to have this new experience. And the beauty was, because other dogs are exercised there every day, they would also get the sensory stimulation of other smells which is something they love on their walks. I felt like my prayers were finally being answered.

When we arrived, certain crucial information had been left out. In order to get to the field, you first have to walk through an enormous meadow full of horses and other dog-walkers. As I sat in the car park watching the heads of other animals bob up from the long grass, I felt crushed. How could they have missed this vital piece of information out! Kiara had already spotted another dog and was kicking off, barking like a crazed animal, which freaked

Otis out so much he joined in. As more dogs and their owners walked into the car park, the more crazed Kiara became. I got out of the car and walked across to the path which led to the field. The gate was so far away I had to squint to even see it. I knew there was absolutely no way I could hold one let alone both dogs to get them past the volume of animals roaming about. I turned and looked at my dogs in the back seat, barking and slathering, stressed out of their minds, and I burst into tears. Yet another hope dashed. Yet another possible solution to my problem gone. I drove straight home, crying from frustration and disappointment both for them and for me.

Thursday 13 June – Vegas Baby!

A bit of escapism is just what I need right now. At the airport, I had a glass of champagne to calm my nerves and a second one to celebrate. Lady Gaga in Vegas, with my best mate – it doesn't get much better than this. I had relinquished all my air miles, from years of saving them up, to upgrade my flight to business class and I was determined to enjoy this experience to the max.

The business lounge, however, was not as expected. The calm oasis of indulgence and decadence I thought I'd be entering was more like walking into a club in Benidorm. Heavily-tattooed, flushed-faced, drunken yobs holding boom boxes filled the lounge. It was so loud it had the unified hum of a football stadium. What were these hooligans doing in business class and how the hell could they afford it? Surely, they hadn't all spent four years collecting air miles on their credit cards?

Everyone was absolutely rat-arsed. Clearly they'd been drinking since breakfast, and boarding the plane was like piling into a nightclub. I felt like I was on the plane with the world's biggest stag do, but actually, it was worse – it was the Big Fight in Vegas tomorrow and travelling on the plane with me was the heavyweight champion's entire entourage and fan club. I was sharing the plane with dozens of pissed-up yobs who filled the whole business-class cabin.

The eight-hour flight was a living nightmare for most passengers and crew, but for me, a nervous flyer, it was a living hell. As the entourage drank the trollies dry, the level of shouting and general abuse became out of control. They were smoking in the toilets and doing god knows what else. I could see the crew were scared to antagonise them as their binge-drinking got worse. And as if that wasn't bad enough, because of the heatwave, we continually hit hot air pockets which caused the most terrifying turbulence during the last four hours of the flight. My hypnotherapy recording was about as helpful as a one-legged man in an arse-kicking contest. I honestly thought I was going to die. As the plane hit a huge air pocket and plummeted, I grabbed the large tattooed arm to my right and was told aggressively, 'Get off, mate. Even my wife ain't as bad as you.'

The only sober person other than myself and a terrified older couple a few rows in front, was the young guy behind me. As the plane came in for the most tumultuous landing, he put a reassuring hand on my shoulder. As we hit the ground, bumping from side to side, he assured me not to worry and convinced me that it was always like this flying into Vegas. When the pilot skidded to a stop and said over the tannoy, *'Phew, that was a close one!'* he squeezed my arm and smiled. I'd never been more grateful for a barefaced lie in all my life.

But at last we were here, alive – just – and in one piece. And more importantly, I could finally get away from this motley crew. As I ran at top speed to the taxi rank to beat the yobbos, a group of the pissed-up blokes were somehow already in the queue. Hiding at the back and hoping not to be spotted, I heard one of them say, 'The Wynn Hotel, mate.' OH MY GOD, you have got to be kidding me! They were only staying at my hotel.

Friday 14 June

Fortunately, hotels in Vegas are so ludicrously big that you had to be really unlucky to bump into someone you knew. And for the first time in a long while, I was actually lucky. I also think I was probably on the opposite time schedule to them so that when I was awake in the day, they would be sleeping off the night before. To be safe, I booked the sophisticated hotel restaurant for lunch as it was unlikely to be the place they'd be at lunchtime. If they were even up by lunchtime, I was sure they would be draining a bar somewhere else.

Lady Gaga was nothing short of phenomenal. A night of cocktails, singing (bellowing) and dancing my rocks off was just what the doctor ordered. It was clear how preoccupied I'd been before coming away when I opened my luggage bag and saw I'd forgotten to pack any tops. I had breakfast in my pyjama top and Maya bought a tour T-shirt which I wore for the rest of the trip. It was a good job I only went for two days as a hotel T-shirt was sixty quid!

In fear of flying back with the entourage and being dead on arrival, I found out which flight they were returning on and managed to swap my flight to a different one. It was quite a different experience on the return flight and I managed to get some shut-eye and enjoy the air miles I'd wasted on the way out!

Saturday 15 June

It was so good to be home with my family. The pups went bananas when they saw me.

I was well aware that Ivan had banked some serious brownie points, and although I'd only been gone seventy-two hours, it felt like a hell of a lot longer than that! The stress of that flight made looking after the pups feel like a day off.

Sunday 16 June – Father's Day

I woke at the crack of dawn and was surprised to have jet lag. I'd barely been in Vegas long enough to register the time difference. I let the pups out as quietly as I could and stayed in the garden with them, collapsing on one of the sun loungers. It was already hot and I felt like a zombie. I hadn't put my contact lenses in yet but I could see something bright green hanging out of Kiara's mouth. I squinted to focus. Oh shit – Ivan's new gardening gloves! I rushed over to retrieve them from between her jaws when I saw a head dangling out of one side. It was a parakeet! Although she was parading around, chuffed with her prey, I could see it had in fact been dead for quite a while as decay was setting in. I was relieved the poor thing hadn't been murdered by her and I was equally thankful the gloves were still in one piece. I went inside to wrap them before Kiara got her beady eyes on those too, and buried the little bird in the compost heap.

Monday 17 June

I met up with an old school friend today who was telling me about her daughter who's just been diagnosed with

Autism. She explained that she doesn't like her routine being changed, has acute anxiety, is hyperactive, can't concentrate, has lots of phobias and is anti-social. A light went off. She sounded exactly like Kiara! Kiara paces if we sit in her spot on the sofa, has to eat her food at the same time in the same place every day. She gets anxious if we change her routine and doesn't like new people and finds it impossible to stay focussed.

I looked up Autism in dogs which miraculously does exist. Kiara had every one of the symptoms; sensitivity to noise, paw licking, chewing, destructive behaviour and avoids eye contact. It was incredible. Of course, it's not recognised by the veterinary profession as most institutions seem to require at least a decade to catch up with what's actually going on in the real world. I seriously think Kiara could be autistic. It would explain so much. I need to find out more...

Tuesday 18 June

Ella asked me today when she'd be able to walk the dogs like her friends do. We all knew the real answer to this question, but I said, 'Maybe when you're older' (and if you're a heavyweight wrestler). I remember the joy of walking Ben when I was Ella's age. It was so liberating and grown up taking your dog out by yourself, but with the strength and unpredictability of these dogs, I don't even let an experienced dog-walker take them out. Otis only listens to me when we're out if I use my "woman possessed" voice, which is so scary it actually gives me a jolt when I use it. A deep gruff command and he knows I mean business. I'm not sure he'd respond to any other voice and so it is not worth the risk.

Kiara is a no go for more reasons than there is space to mention.

Wednesday 19 June

After another major growth spurt, Otis's neck is now the thickness of a Redwood. I wasn't sure his regular nylon collar could take a lunging without snapping in half.

I'm scrapping the harness altogether as he's nearly a year and all it does is signal to him to take off as fast as he can. I'd read that in America, large dogs wore choke chain collars but the reviews in the UK made them sound like torture devices and it would be tantamount to animal cruelty. I read one of the top trainers in the US uses something called a prong collar but I think that guy is now in jail.

I called the local training centre to ask their advice. They were against any collar whatsoever and insisted I continue to use a harness so that it doesn't hurt his neck. This was all very well except for the fact that I could be dragged under a truck if he spotted a squirrel across the road. I thanked them for their useless advice and hung up. I settled for a collar which was three-quarters robust material with a small chain of a few inches. This would give a little tug if he pulled but apparently just the sound of the chain was usually enough to stop dogs pulling.

I think I'll practise with it in the park before I head out into the streets. Better to be safe than dead.

Friday 21 June – Kiara's assessment

I'm taking Kiara for her psychological assessment today. Despite the locum having a good old guffaw at my suggestion that she might be Autistic, as far as I was aware, I didn't think, *she definitely isn't the full ticket*, was a medical diagnosis. While Otis is learning and developing and, dare I say, maturing, Kiara isn't – and I need a specialist's opinion. There is still so much we don't understand about animals and just because it's not in a text book, does not mean it doesn't exist. I needed somebody with an open mind and Penny recommended someone she thought could help.

I am greeted by a handsome young Italian man in a white coat which is already reassuring. He is a qualified vet and a dog psychologist. But more importantly, he is gentle and kind and has one of those demeanours that when they ask how you are, you can't help but start crying. I feel emotional before I've even entered the consulting room. He is so softly spoken that I have to strain to hear him. He has an Italian lilt which makes him even more removed from the blinkered opinions of a lot of "experts" I've met over the past year. Even though I could see Kiara was scared, I felt safe knowing she was in good hands with this gentle stranger.

'As she is very nervous,' he said softly, 'I am just going to sit over here until she gets used to me.' He moved to a chair across the room. I didn't like to say that it could take all day and his other clients might have something to say about this.

He held out a treat for Kiara but she stayed by the door, tail tucked under her bottom, shaking.

Instinctively I pulled her towards me to reassure her.

'Just stay where you are,' he said kindly. '*She* will come to *you* if she needs comfort.' He sounded like a wise sage twice his age.

'Now, tell me your concerns,' he said.

I took a deep breath and went into detail about her anxiety, her impulsive behaviour and destructive nature. He listened without interrupting once as it all poured out of me. It sounded so incongruous with her standing there, quietly shaking like a leaf. She didn't look like she was capable of hurting a fly.

'She doesn't like any change in her routine, and as you

can see, she is very scared of strangers.' He nodded. 'And she's not trainable,' I added. He watched her for a long time, observing and analysing.

'She is very beautiful,' he said. I wasn't expecting him to say this and had to bite my lip not to cry.

'So, she needs routine, love and a lot of patience, yes?' he said. I nodded as I didn't trust my voice not to crack as the emotion of the last ten months rose up like a tsunami.

He looked straight at me and said, 'She is a dog with special needs and you meet those needs. She is very lucky to have you.' My eyes filled with tears and I dare not blink.

He surmised that Kiara has very high levels of cortisol, which she's probably had from birth. This means she is constantly in a state of fight or flight which explains her overreaction to minor things. He said we could pay a small fortune for a brain scan which would only show us what we already know. We both agreed that tranquilizers were not the way to go as I didn't want her to be spaced out, just to be calmer and happy. He prescribed some medication that would help lower her cortisol levels but wouldn't sedate her in any way.

'They will either work or do absolutely nothing,' he said. 'Either way, you will know in two to four weeks.'

In the meantime, he suggested exposing her very gradually to what she is afraid of, and rewarding her, but not to push it. We should continue giving her a routine for security and not to feel that her life is compromised as she doesn't need the same things that other dogs do. She has a big garden for exercise, a loving family for comfort and her brother to play with. She only needs a walk a couple of times a week.

Then he got me. 'It is very difficult to deal with a dog with this behaviour. In most cases, she would be rehomed and probably put to sleep, but she chose you because *you* are exactly what she needs.' After my monumental effort to keep my emotions in check, I cracked. The dam broke and the tears came flooding out. Just as he finished talking, Kiara walked over to him, sat down and gave him her paw and took the treat he'd been holding all this time.

Monday 24 June

I called E and explained what had been going on with Kiara and asked whether there had been any problems with any of the puppies at birth.

'Four of the puppies were stillborn,' E said. 'Several hours after nine of the puppies were born, we heard wailing and went downstairs. We saw that four more puppies had been born but were all stillborn. We Googled how to resuscitate them and brought them all back to life.'

And there it was. She said that Kiara wasn't one of them, but how could she possibly know when all thirteen of them were in a pen together and looked identical. If Kiara was one of the stillborn puppies, it would explain everything. None of this behaviour was her fault and she was unlikely to ever change. We had to do our best to make things work, for her and for us.

Wednesday 26 June

Watching Kiara on the sofa reacting to any movement in the garden makes me realise how stressful everyday life must be for her. To be in a constant state of high alert must be so exhausting. I've made a list of adjustments we can do to help her life be as stress-free as possible:

- walks on lead at quiet times of the day
- move her bed away from the window

- close living room curtains early evening to shut out stimuli
- keep toys nearby for her to chew at all times
- put her away when people come to visit who she doesn't know
- keep volume levels low so she doesn't get triggered
- extra naps in her crate so she can switch off
- play classical music during the day to calm her down

Even if the pills don't work, I feel more positive now that we know why she behaves this way. If we adapt our behaviour to suit her needs, by putting these simple changes into place, I'm sure things will start to improve.

Friday 28 June

I'm following the advice of the lovely Italian vet by desensitising Kiara to everyday stimuli when we're out walking. I'm rewarding her with her favourite biscuits each time she sees a bird or squirrel on the path and doesn't bark or lunge. She is doing so well with this bird/biscuit association that now, whenever she sees a bird, she expects a treat. This applies even when she sees a bird flying overhead or sitting in a tree. She stops dead in her tracks and looks at me, waiting for her treat. I am effectively treating her for bird watching. If this continues, she'll be so overweight she won't be able to leave the house to spot anything. I switch to rewarding her with praise instead but this doesn't prove nearly as effective, so I break the biscuits into tiny pieces and give her these. Remarkably, it doesn't matter how small the treats are – it's the gesture that seems to count. Wouldn't it be lovely if humans were the same way. Understanding her is making it so much easier to deal with her and I finally feel like we are making progress, which I was doubting was ever possible. And best of all, she seems so much happier.

CHAPTER 12 – JULY

TURNING ONE YEAR OLD – A BIRTHDAY TO REMEMBER!

Weight: Otis 43 kg / Kiara 38 kg

Monday 1 July

Kiara begins her meds today. The chill pills have been sitting in the cupboard like little rays of hope while I've been counting down the days 'til she can start them. We're all praying for a miracle but keeping expectations realistic since the specialist said they may do zilch.

Of course, nothing is ever straightforward with Kiara. Her weight is right in between doses which means she needs to have three-quarters of a pill each night. The pills are the size of a five-pence piece and are on the Mohs Hardness scale of a diamond. There is only one shallow score to break the pill in half and there is no utensil in the house which can break the pill into quarters. We'd need a hacksaw to cut the pill successfully.

Unlike cats, dogs are pretty laid back when it comes to taking medicine. To get a cat to take a pill requires the skill of a master chemist in order to disguise the taste and smell of the foreign substance. It can take multiple attempts and several hours to trick a cat into eating even a sprinkling of a pill you've crushed to dust and mixed in with their favourite food. Dogs, on the other hand, tend to eat anything that doesn't eat them first. Stick a pill in their bowl and they'll gobble it down with dinner, none the wiser. Some dogs will even take the pill straight from you, thinking it's a treat, before realising they've taken medicine. But not Kiara. After she'd licked her bowl sparkling clean, the three pieces of broken pill were left stuck to the sides of the bowl. Just as I was about to get the hammer to smash them to smithereens and mix them with some wet food, Otis ate them. I will try again tomorrow.

Tuesday 2 July

It's going to hit 90 degrees today. Kiara, being the sun worshipper of the household, lies in the sunny spot on the garden sofa but can only manage a few minutes before her nose is streaming and she's heavily panting. Even these African descendants can't handle a British heatwave. Otis has chosen the more sensible option of lying on the grass in the shade. But Kiara, once cooled off indoors, comes back out and lies in the full midday sun. She is actually hot to the touch.

The pups had their last weigh-in at the vets and I'm relieved that they won't get much bigger now. Kiara weighs more than Ella, at 38 kilos, and Otis isn't far off my weight at 43 kilos. Compared to when we got them, it seems crazy they are the weight of their human family at just a year old.

I took Otis out wearing his new collar. I walked the entire way with him at "heel", and he didn't growl at any passing dogs. I rewarded him with treats every time he walked to heel and every time he saw a dog and didn't snarl, and he seemed chuffed to bits with himself. Amazingly, the three packets of treats didn't spoil his appetite for dinner which he happily scoffed down. I add water to his food to slow him down so he doesn't get bloat which is common (and fatal) in large dogs who eat their food like it's the last meal they'll ever have. Ironically, Kiara eats in such a civilised manner compared to Otis. Now that the pups are one year old, their meals can be cut down to two feeds a day – breakfast and dinner. A much more civilised routine for all.

Wednesday 3 July

We're taking Mum to the Hampton Court Flower Show and Jane is coming to look after the pups. It's so hot they are too zonked to get into mischief so it should be an easy sit for Jane. I've set up fans around the house to keep them cool but they only lie in the rooms without the fans where it's boiling hot. I've bought them some ice-lollies which they love, so that should keep them cool.

I noticed this morning that Otis's head is almost touching the top of his crate when he sits up so I'll need to get a bigger one soon. Kiara still has a way to go. Even though there's only five kilos between them, their physiques are entirely different. Otis is broad with rippling muscles and a large head. His chest measurement is more than a metre now. Kiara is slim and petit but you can see without a shadow of a doubt that they are brother and sister. Even though Otis has an endless amount of expressions and Kiara only two – cute and confused – their faces resemble each other's and they are the most stunning dogs I've ever seen. I know parents with an ugly baby always think it's beautiful, but in this case, I know it is absolutely true. The most beautiful are always the most difficult.

Thursday 4 July

As a special treat for the pups' first birthday and to celebrate the fact that:

1. I'm still alive
2. Ivan hasn't filed for divorce
3. my family are still talking to me (well most of them)
4. we haven't been taken to court (by neighbours, Royal Mail or other dog owners),

we are taking the pups to the New Forest for a long birthday weekend. They seem as excited about the news as Ella is. Although, as long as they are with us, they'd be happy going to the tip for the weekend. But this is a landmark moment for all of us and needs to be celebrated. One whole year (which has aged me a decade) without giving up is certainly something to be proud of.

Friday 5 July – Off to the New Forest

We need two cars – one for the dogs and one for the luggage. The dogs and Ella travel with me – Ella in the front and Otis and Kiara in the back. Given their size now, they need to be considerate of each other and curl up on the back seat in order for them to both fit in. This doesn't happen. Otis spent the journey on the floor, wedged between the front and back seat, while Kiara was spread-eagled across the entire back seat. Ella spent her time trying to detangle their seatbelts to prevent them strangling themselves.

Luckily, Kiara had worn herself out by barking at everything for the whole journey so by the time we arrived in the New Forest, she was asleep and blissfully unaware of the wild donkeys and ponies peering into her window.

After spending a vast amount of time and money searching for the perfect dog-friendly cottage, we realised on arrival that our version of "dog-friendly" did not coincide with the travel company's definition. The fencing around the garden was essentially two slats which the dogs had the choice of either jumping over or limbo-ing under. We had to use the garden furniture to block off the fence which meant we only had one sun lounger to share between the five of us. Naturally, Kiara bagsied it.

Unloading all the pups' paraphernalia took an age. We set up their crates and beds like at home so they felt secure. As we lugged all their things into the cottage, they both conked out on the sofa. A quick look at the guest handbook opened with "Please do not allow dogs on the furniture" so I shooed them off and brushed off what I realised was another dog's fur. I looked behind the cushions and the sofa was covered in dog hair – not belonging to my two – so I signalled for them to get back on.

A balmy evening with the sun setting over the forest was absolute paradise. Until the neighbour's dog started barking and Otis and Kiara ran around the garden trying to locate the best vantage point to outbark it.

As the sun was setting, we took the pups for a walk in the forest, Otis off lead and Kiara on a long lead. After the initial excitement of them being together and Otis tangling himself up in Kiara's lead, they settled down and walked properly. I'd chosen a remote area, cut off from the nearest town so no other dog-walkers were around. It was so peaceful and we were all very impressed at how well they behaved. We came back to the cottage, proud and happy that finally these mad dogs were becoming less of a menace to society and more of a joy to take out. I put them both to bed, switched on their bedtime music and they went straight off to sleep.

We sat outside, squashed together on the sun lounger, and raised a toast to our first holiday with the dogs. Ella was so excited and after exploring the property in-depth, including the cesspit, joined us. It was so beautiful and I felt remarkably relaxed and full of hope for the future.

Saturday 6 July – Otis's and Kiara's First Birthday!

The pups are one year old today! To celebrate their birthday, I bought an expensive bottle of champagne which I cracked open at 11 a.m. To celebrate their birthday, the pups ate the sun lounger.

After breakfast, we took them for a walk to the same spot we'd been to last night. They were so excited to be walking together – it was really sweet. I could see how happy this made Ella too. We finally felt like a normal family taking their dogs out for a family walk. We kept Kiara on lead as Otis ran over to Ella who had found a makeshift swing hanging from one of the trees.

When the coast was clear, we decided to let Kiara off lead and let them have a play together as it was their birthday. Otis's recall is now 100% and Kiara's has been really good lately. We reached a large clearing and with no one in sight, Ivan let Kiara off. I held my breath as she tore off, Otis only just able to keep up with her. As she ripped around the trees at breakneck speed, she looked like she'd never been let out before. When I called them, they both came racing back to me which filled me with a confidence I'd not had before. We put Kiara back on the lead and walked further into the forest. When we came to another clearing, Ivan suggested we let them have another run together so they would be tired and sleep when we went for lunch. I felt this might be pushing it, but they had behaved so well and there was no one around. I unclicked Kiara's harness and she tore into the distance, took a left turn and disappeared out of sight. Otis was right behind her.

The grass was so long I couldn't see or hear either of them. We called them but nothing. Way off in the distance I could see a stampede of horses and the faint sound of a dog barking. It was unmistakably Kiara. I ran as fast as I could in that direction, calling for Otis and Kiara, but the herd was moving further away, towards the main road. At this point, I dropped everything and was screaming their names, running like my life depended on it. I was filled with complete dread and panic. I knew they would reach the road at any second and that they would be killed, along with who knows how many horses. It was my worst nightmare. A woman came running out of her house with a lasso.

'WE NEED TO CATCH THEM BEFORE THE RANGERS SHOOT THEM,' she yelled, running with me. Rangers have the legal right to shoot a dog if they think a horse is in danger. Horrific images flashed through my mind. Ivan was screaming after them and Ella was crying, and I was just running as fast as my legs would carry me.

Then I heard a sound which made my heart stop – the sound of hooves on the road. I ran even faster. In the distance, like a mirage, I saw a blurry flash of auburn over the top of the towering grass and I knew it was Otis trying to find us. He was darting around in different directions and I could only catch glimpses of him now and then above the long grass. Otis spotted the woman with the lasso and ran towards her, thinking it was me. I called out to him and he charged in my direction. He was out of his mind with stress, foaming at the mouth and shaking. Then from out of the tall grass, Kiara appeared. I could hear the sound of hooves on the tarmac slowing down and was relieved no one had got killed. Ivan was shaking. He was understandably livid and grabbed hold of the dogs.

'Don't shout at them,' I said firmly. I took both dogs and clicked them onto their leads. 'I'll walk them back.' And I calmly walked both stressed-out dogs back to the cottage.

I let them drink all the water they needed, which seemed like gallons, and put them in their crates. I didn't say a word to them or give them any eye contact. Ivan was shaking his head and was beside himself.

'They are Rhodesian Ridgebacks,' I said. 'They are lion chasers – this is what they do.' I understood his anger at what could have ended in catastrophic disaster.

'We can't punish them for their DNA,' I said. 'This is not their fault. It's ours.'

'Come on, let's go for lunch.'

We walked out to the car and I put my arm around Ella who was still upset.

'By the way,' I said to Ivan, 'you're driving.'

We drove to The Pig Hotel where we were having lunch and I ordered the strongest cocktail they had on the menu. It tasted like pure meths which was exactly what I needed.

'Rough morning?' the barman asked.

'More like a rough year,' I replied.

'You have no idea,' said Ivan with his head in his hands.

As the cocktails kicked in and the adrenalin dispersed, I counted my blessings that no one had been hurt. I could see Ella and Ivan were disheartened that all the hard work I'd put into the dogs had been undone. I kicked myself for being foolish enough to let two hunting dogs off lead in an area with wild animals. It was a stupid, reckless mistake, but we were not back to where we started. We had gone a few steps backwards, that's all.

These were my dogs, my responsibility, and part of the family. I had a duty to take care of them in the very best way that I could. Never again would I be so irresponsible.

I had learnt a very important lesson and one I will never forget. No matter how well you train a dog, they are still a dog and you will never quash their instinctive nature. And nor should you try.

After lunch we headed back to the cottage, and to two bouncing balls of energy who behaved like nothing had ever happened. Our nerves might be shot to pieces but for them, it was a regular afternoon of us returning home and them being overjoyed to see us, like they always are. One of the best things about dogs is that they just live in the moment. There is no regret, no hard feelings, no prolonged guilt or shame – they are not wired to feel that way. Like all animals, they simply understand happiness, love, fear and loss. And they feel each of these emotions to the absolute max.

We celebrated their first year in this world with the gusto they deserved. Music, dancing, singing, treats and oodles of hugs and kisses, and they relished every second of it. Although I knew I still had another year to go until they calmed down, things could only get better from here (fingers tightly crossed).

I don't know whether an experience like today's would teach them never to do it again, but I sure as hell wasn't going to find out!

Next year, to celebrate their birthday, we'll go to the Outer Hebrides or a remote island without any inhabitants (certainly no wild horses). Or maybe we'll just celebrate at home and buy them a couple of sun loungers.

EPILOGUE

Revised House Rules

1. Dogs now own the sofa
2. Dogs are allowed on beds, *when invited*
3. Dogs are allowed crisps, crumpets with peanut butter on weekends and cake on birthdays (we seem to have a lot of birthdays)
4. Dogs are still not allowed to eat food from the table (even when we're not looking)
5. Dogs are still not allowed to chew the furniture (including sun loungers)
6. Dogs must not jump up (with the exception of Jane, Gemma and Amber)
7. Dogs can only bark in the garden when playing together

N.B. Although Kiara thinks rules are made to be broken, the above apply to both Otis *and* Kiara.

ACKNOWLEDGEMENTS

Being an indie author means you are the writer, agent, editor, designer, production manager, quality controller, marketer and distributor. It isn't so much like climbing a mountain as scaling a vertical rockface whilst having beer cans thrown at you! I could not have done it without the help and support of my family, friends and a team of amazing (and very patient) professionals. I would especially like to thank the following peeps:

Jericho Writers for their continued support and sense of community. Anna Caig for being the lighthouse in the storm and for being a wicked marketeer. Vanessa Mendozzi for my gorgeous book cover. Euan Monaghan for the beautiful interior. Suzanne Sherman, Marnie Summerfield Smith, Debbie Young and Julie Hoyle for their professional coaching and editing.

Andy who taught me to prioritise writing over household chores (who cares if you have to wear the same pants twice). Oliver who wisely told me, 'If monkeys can write I'm sure you can!' Antonia who supported me through my puppy troubles and always found the right thing to say (and who also has a mad dog – more of this later). Maya who listened patiently to my daily frustrations and rants during the writing and production process and was my partner in crime in Vegas baby! Frances who taught me not to be afraid.

Jane, Gemma, Stuart and my folks for lovingly looking after the pups. Ella for her unwavering belief that I could do this! Ti amo Boo. Ivan for not divorcing me over the lawn and for eventually falling in love with the pups. All my amazing friends and family who have continued to show/ feign interest when I've harped on about the book.

To our neighbours, postman, Royal Mail and countless dog experts, my sincere apologies.

And last, but not least, Otis and Kiara without whom this book would not exist and who have taught me that from chaos comes growth (and a helluva lot of wrinkles!).

SAZ'S BIO

by Otis and Kiara

Our mum is the best! She cares about the world and all the animals in it, even when they're naughty like we are sometimes (okay, a lot of the time). She used to live in LA and worked in film and TV but chucked that all in so she could bring up our human sister and be a devoted mama.

This worked out very well for us because now she works from home as a writer and we can spend all day with her, chewing her pencils, helping her finish her lunch and going in and out of her garden office – sometimes twenty times a day!

In the evening Mummy likes watching TV with our human sister and always shares her crisps with us.

She loves ice-skating and going for walks, and even when it's pouring with rain she still takes us out. I think that means she loves us, a lot.

Our mum's dream is to open an animal sanctuary so she can take care of as many animals as possible. She says that's why she's writing this book.

Our mum wants to thank everyone who buys a copy of our book because they will each be a part of the opening of The Gentle Soul Sanctuary.

We hope this diary paints us in a good light... apparently, we weren't the best-behaved puppies!

A BIG THANK YOU!

Please help spread the word far and wide about the book by:

1. Leaving a (fabulous) review today – it *really* helps!
2. Telling the next person you meet, know or spot with a dog to buy this book.
3. Join my mailing list to find out if Kiara's meds kicked in… and for more updates on life with the pups and of course, progress on the sanctuary at **www.sazwilson.com**

Follow me and tag me in a photo with you and your pooch on Instagram **@sazandpups**

Also, you can drop me a "hello" on my website and tell me about your own mad dog stories. I'd love to post them in my newsletter.

Thank you and much love,

Saz & Pups x